EASY PIANO

CHART HITS

2015-2016

ISBN 978-1-4950-5869-1

HAL•LEONARD®
CORPORATION

7777 W. BLUEMOUND RD. P.O. BOX 13819 MILWAUKEE, WI 53213

Visit Hal Leonard Online at
www.halleonard.com

ADVENTURE OF A LIFETIME

Words and Music by GUY BERRYMAN,
JON BUCKLAND, CHRIS MARTIN,
WILL CHAMPION, MIKKEL ERIKSEN
and TOR HERMANSEN

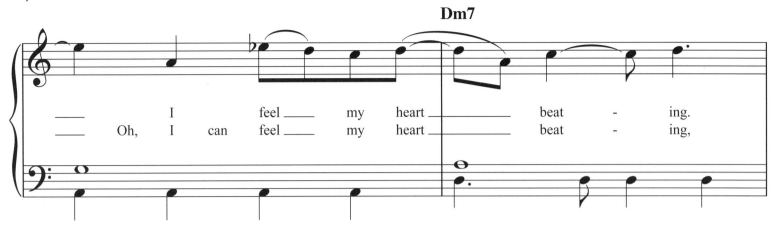

I feel ____ my heart _____ beat - ing.
Oh, I can feel ____ my heart _____ beat - ing,

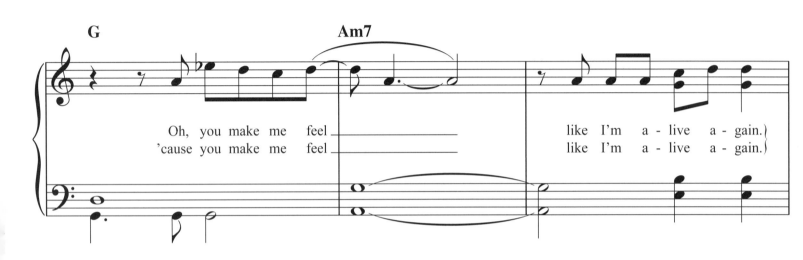

Oh, you make me feel _____ like I'm a - live a - gain.)
'cause you make me feel _____ like I'm a - live a - gain.)

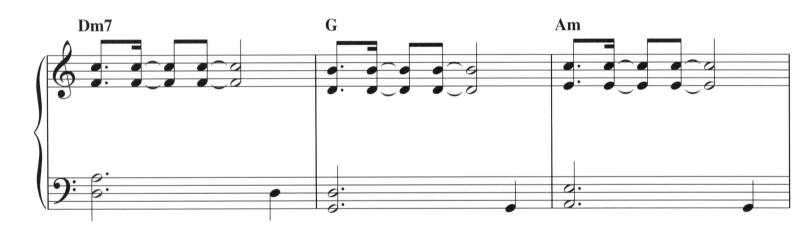

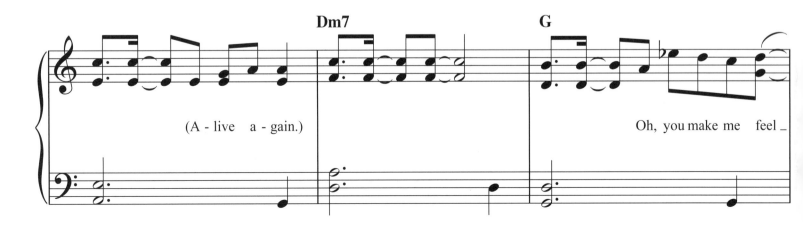

(A - live a - gain.)   Oh, you make me feel _

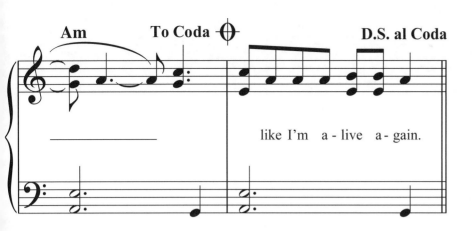

like I'm a - live a - gain.

like I'm a - live a - gain.

"Turn your mag - ic on for me," she'd

say. "Ev - 'ry - thing you want's a dream a - way. Un - der this

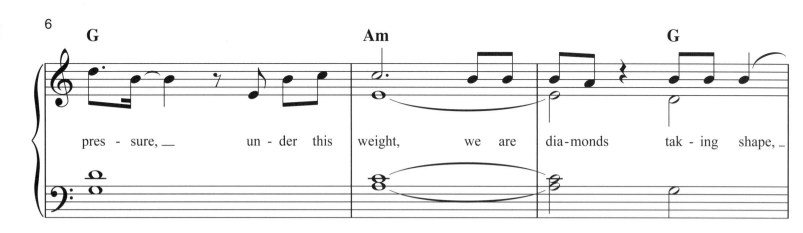

pres - sure, __ un - der this weight, we are dia-monds tak - ing shape, __

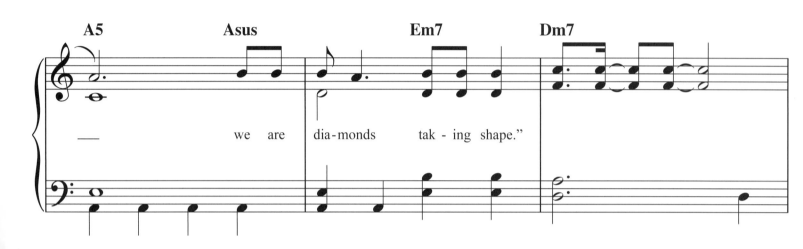

__ we are dia-monds tak - ing shape."

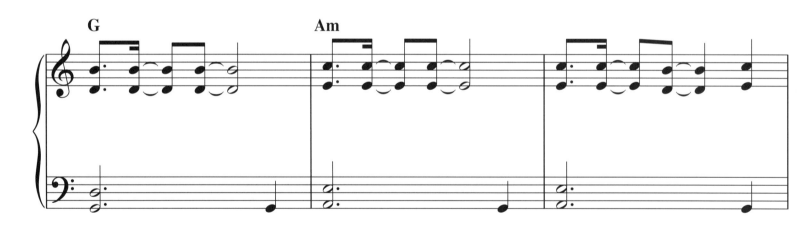

If we've on - ly got this life ___ and this ad -

ven - ture, oh, then I... ___ And if we've on - ly got this life, ___

___ you'll get me through, oh. ___ And if we've on - ly got this life ___

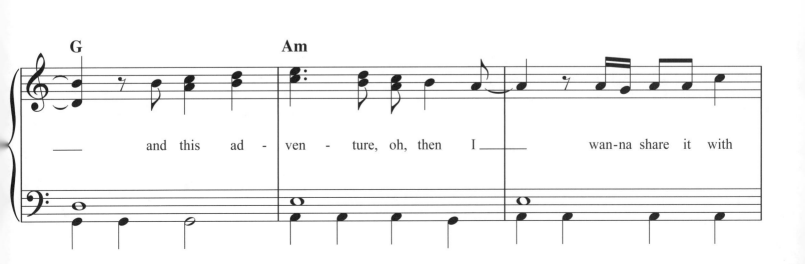

___ and this ad - ven - ture, oh, then I ___ wan-na share it with

CAN'T FEEL MY FACE

Words and Music by ABEL TESFAYE,
MAX MARTIN, SAVAN KOTECHA,
PETER SVENSSON and ALI PAYAMI

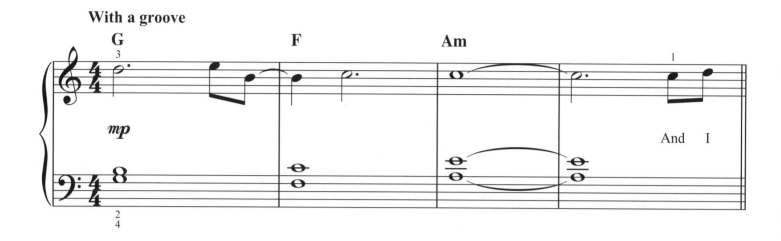

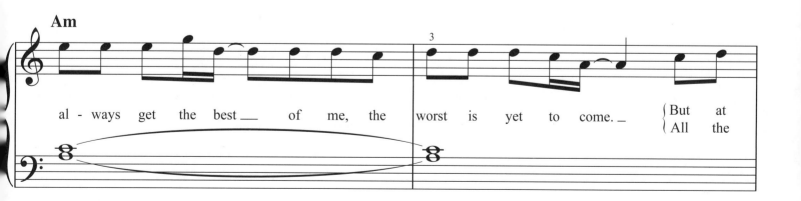

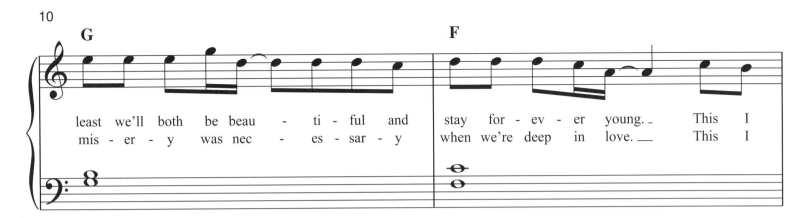

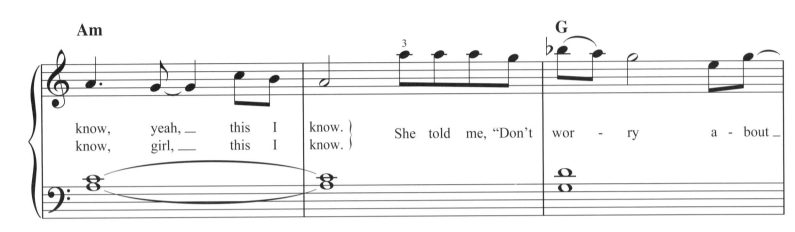

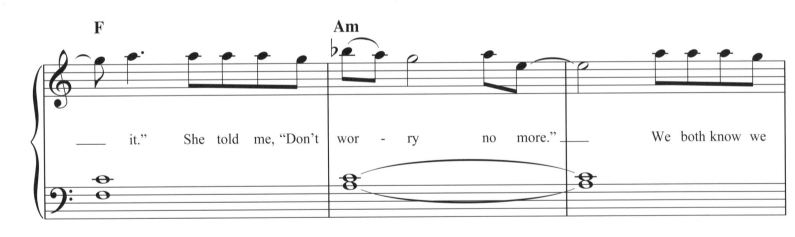

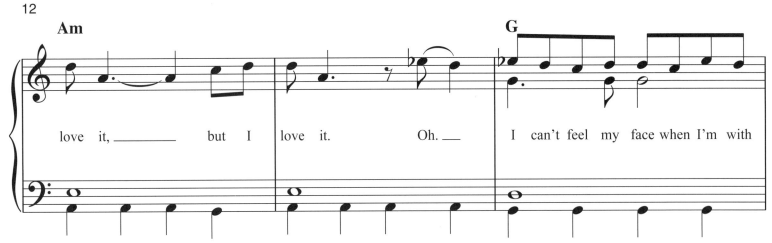

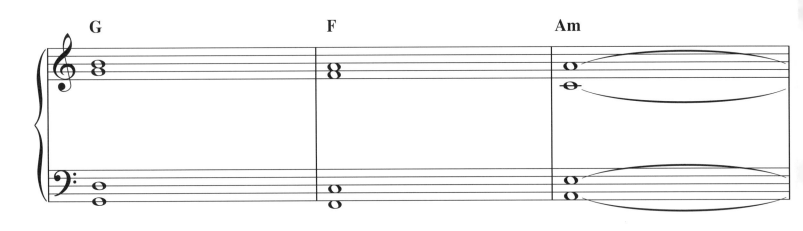

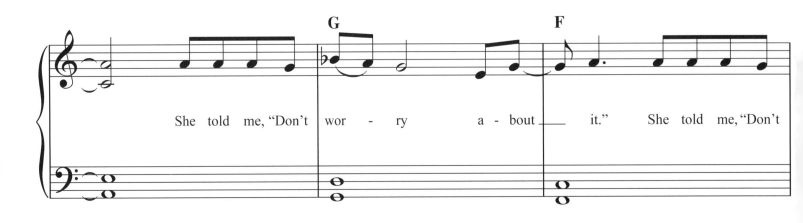

BURNING HOUSE

Words and Music by JEFF BHASKER,
TYLER SAM JOHNSON and CAMARON OCHS

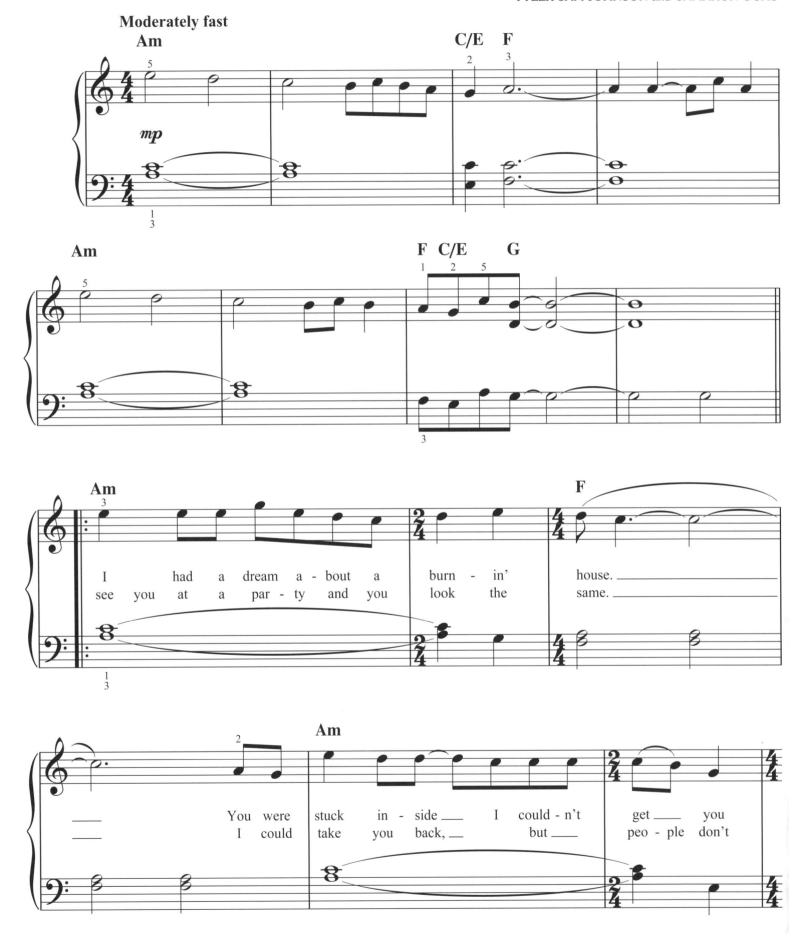

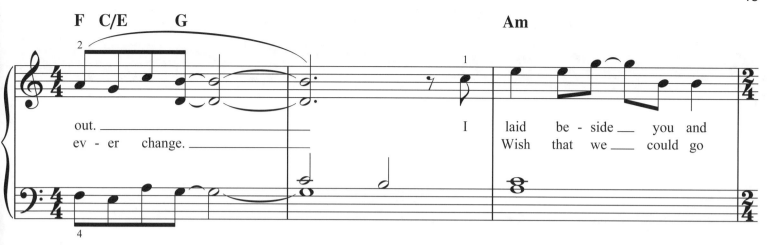

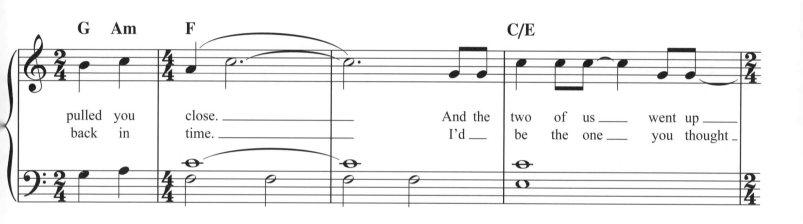

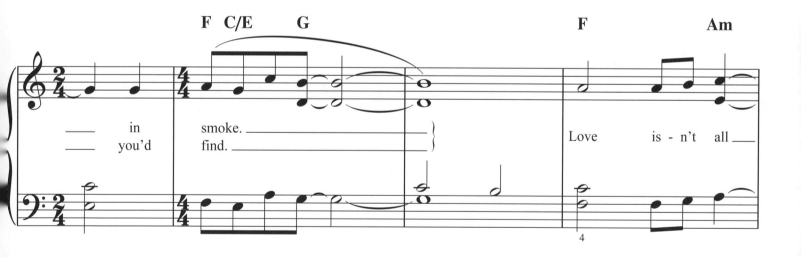

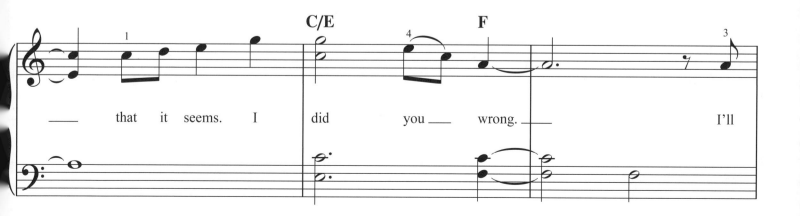

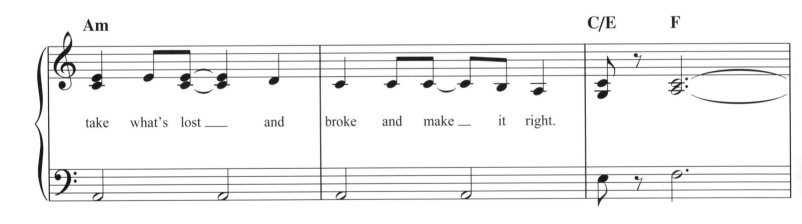

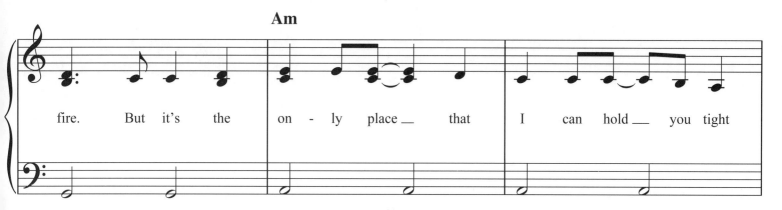

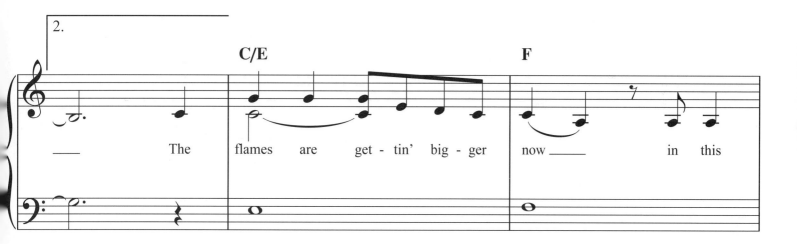

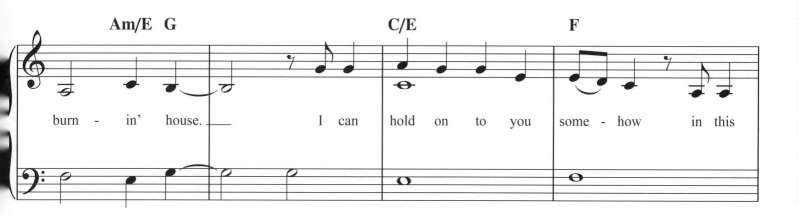

burn - in' house. Oh, and I don't wan - na

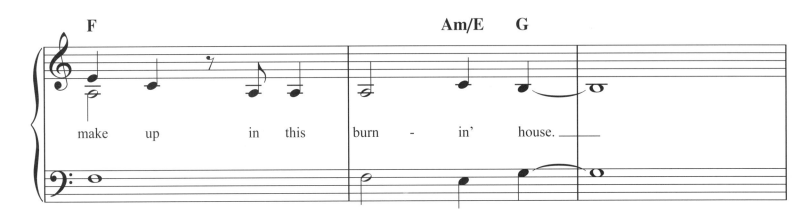

make up in this burn - in' house.

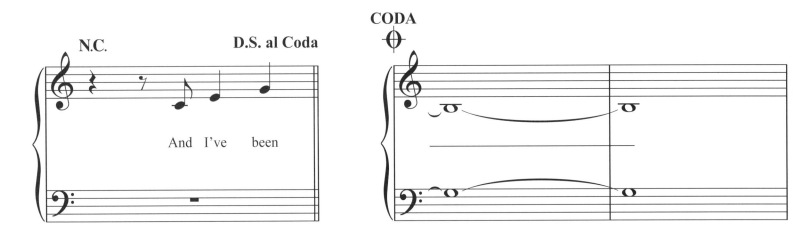

And I've been

CODA

HERE

Words and Music by ALESSIA CARACCIOLO,
WARREN FELDER, ISAAC HAYES,
COLERIDGE TILLMAN, ANDREW WANSEL,
ROBERT GERONGCO, SAMUEL GERONGCO
and TERENCE LAM

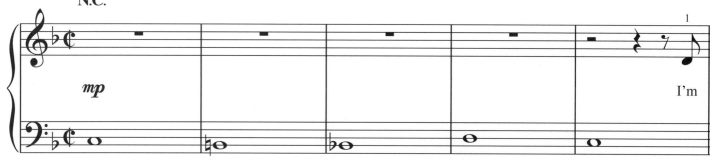

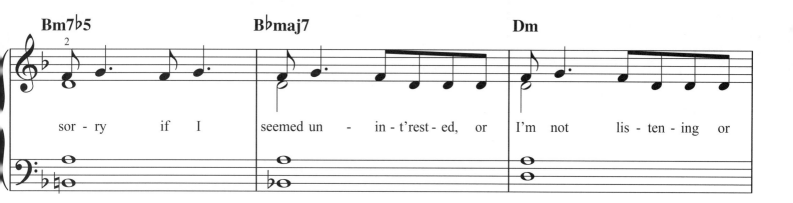

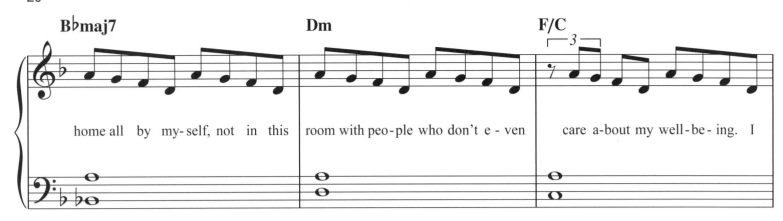

home all by my-self, not in this room with peo-ple who don't e - ven care a-bout my well-be - ing. I

don't dance; don't ask. I don't need a boy-friend, so you can go back.

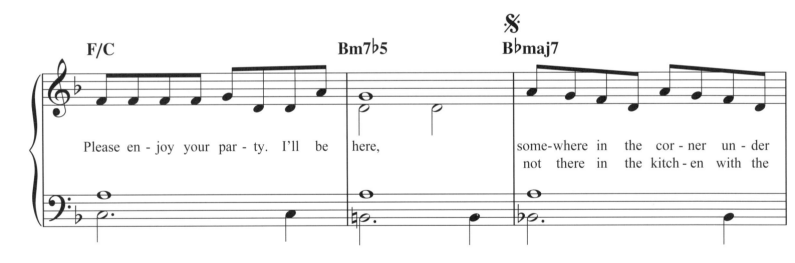

Please en - joy your par - ty. I'll be here, some-where in the cor - ner un-der
not there in the kitch - en with the

clouds of mar - i - jua - na with this boy who's hol - lerin'. I can't hard - ly
girl who's al - ways gos - sip - ing a - bout her friends. So tell them I'll be

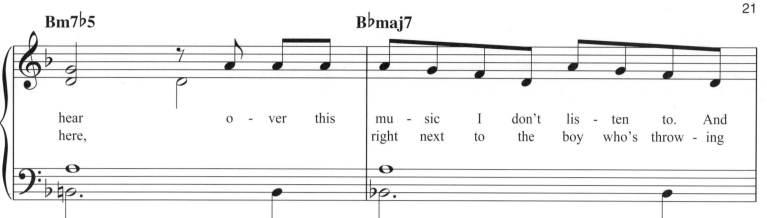

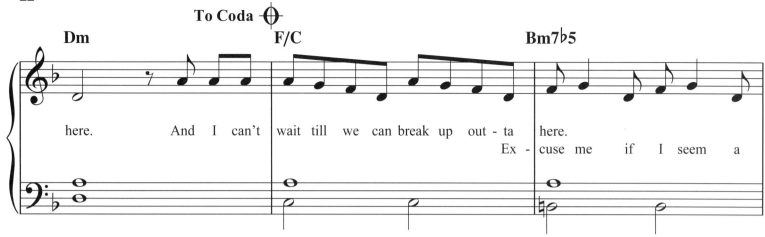

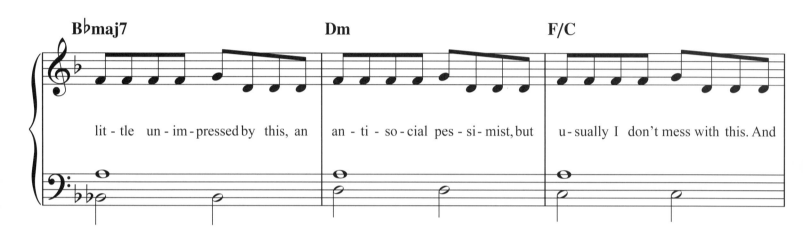

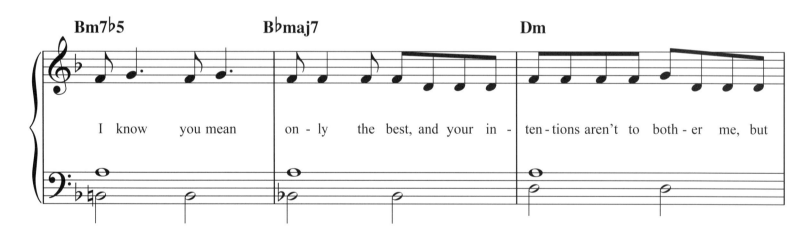

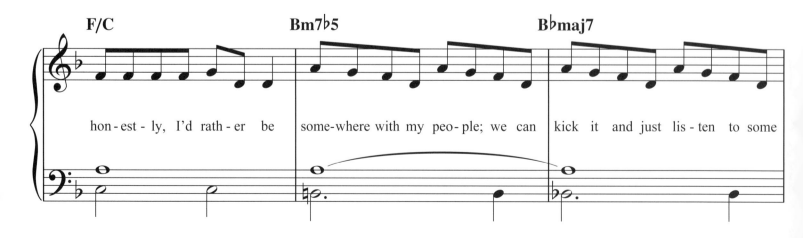

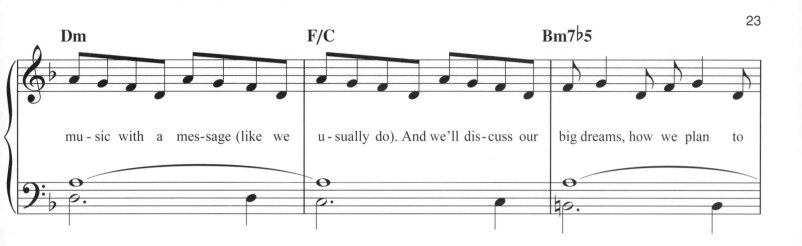

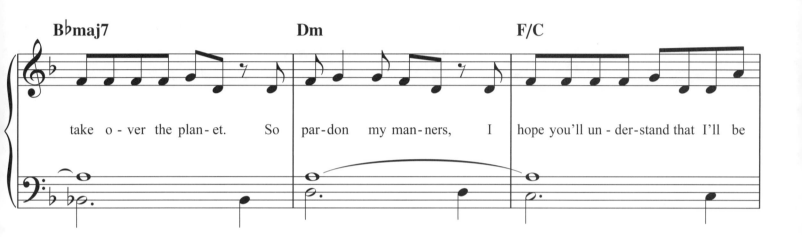

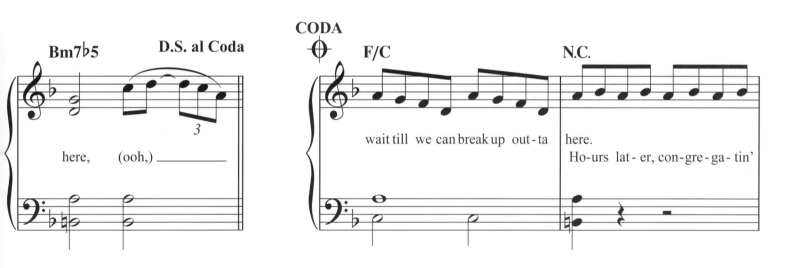

did it ev-er come to this? I should-a nev-er come to this. So hol-ler at me, I'll be in the

car when you're done. I'm stand-off-ish, don't want what you're of-f'ring, and I'm done

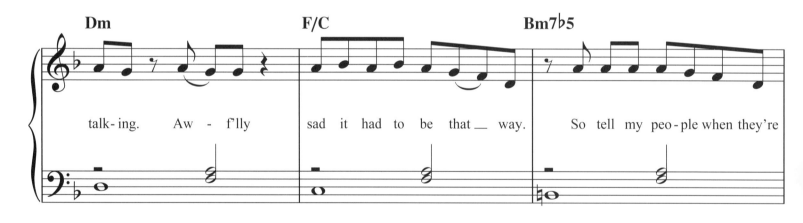

talk-ing. Aw-f'lly sad it had to be that ___ way. So tell my peo-ple when they're

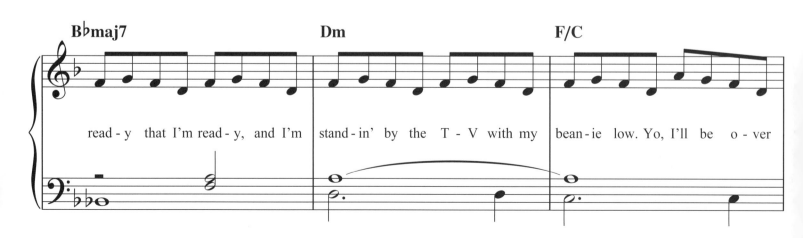

read-y that I'm read-y, and I'm stand-in' by the T-V with my bean-ie low. Yo, I'll be o-ver

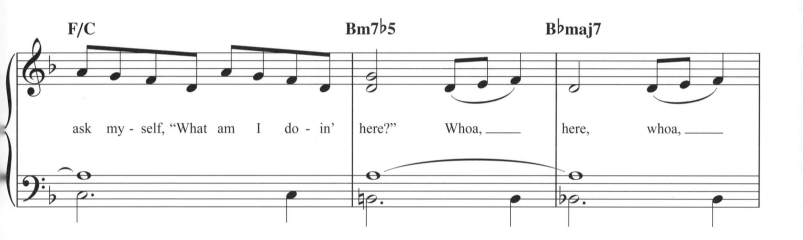

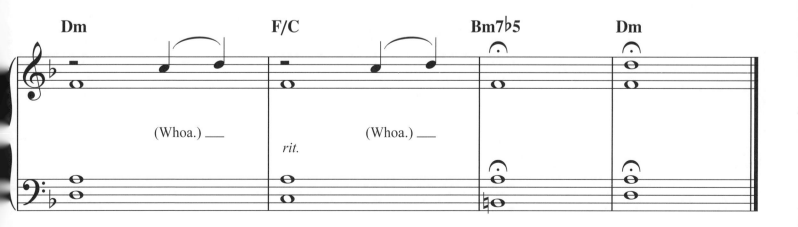

EX'S & OH'S

Words and Music by TANNER SCHNEIDER
and DAVE BASSETT

then I let him ___ go.
how the sea - sons go by.

Now, there's one in Cal - i - for - nia who's been
I ___ get ___ high ___ and I

curs - ing my name ___ 'cause I found me a bet - ter lov - er
love to get low, ___ so the hearts ___ keep ___ break - ing and the

in the U. K., ___ hey, hey, ___ un - til I made my get - a -
heads ___ just roll. ___ You know ___ that's how the sto - ry ___

HELLO

Words and Music by ADELE ADKINS
and GREG KURSTIN

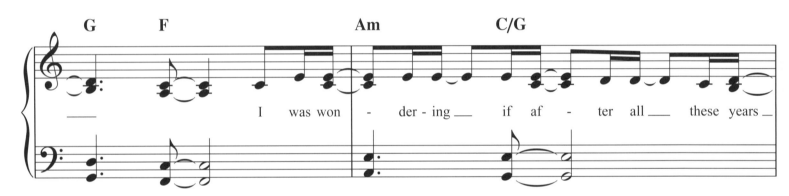

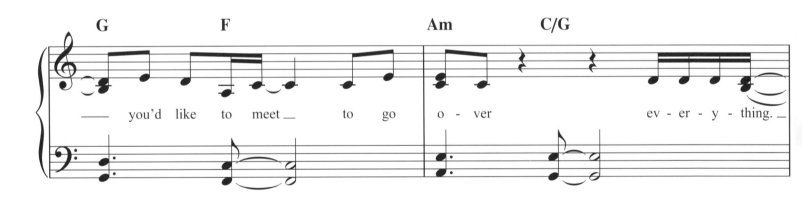

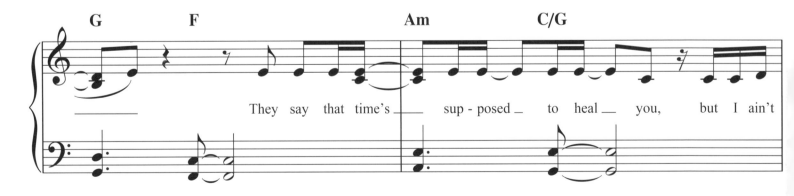

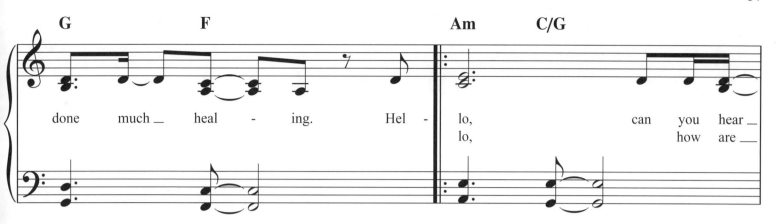

done much __ heal - ing. Hel - lo, can you hear __
lo, how are __

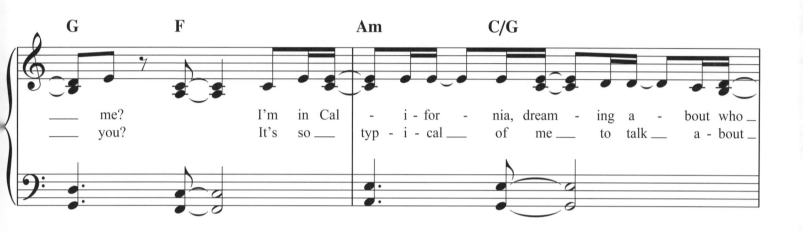

__ me? I'm in Cal - i - for - nia, dream - ing a - bout who __
__ you? It's so __ typ - i - cal __ of me __ to talk __ a - bout __

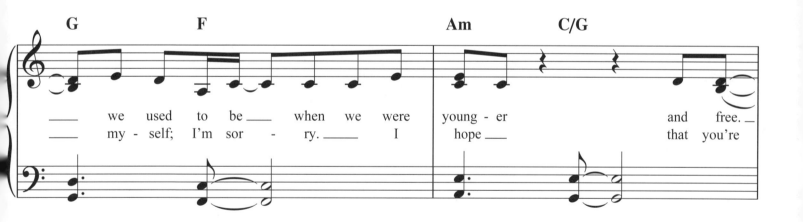

__ we used to be __ when we were young - er and free.
__ my - self; I'm sor - ry. __ I hope __ that you're

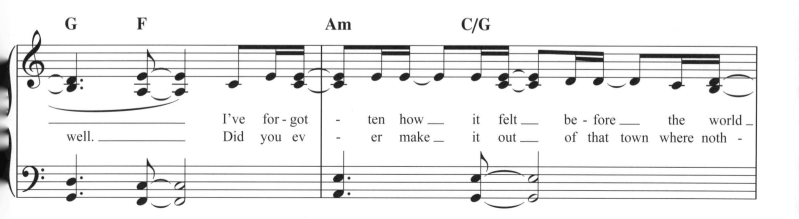

__ well. __ I've for - got - ten how __ it felt __ be - fore __ the world __
well. __ Did you ev - er make __ it out __ of that town where noth -

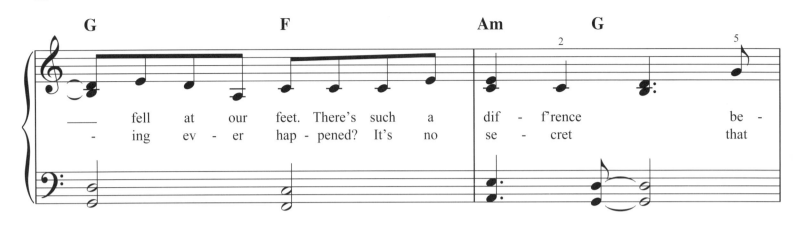

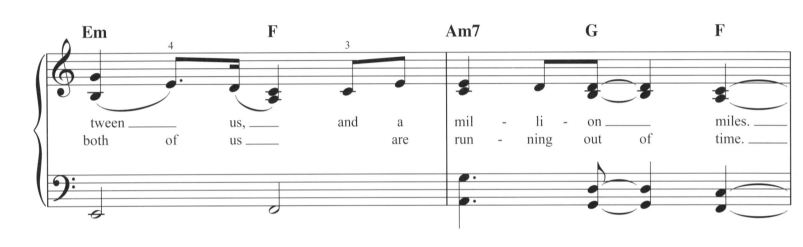

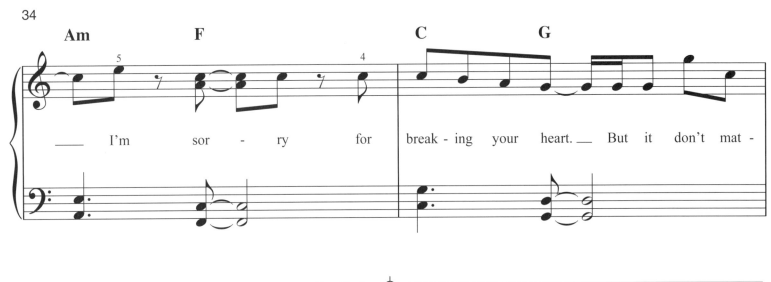

I'm sor - ry for break - ing your heart. __ But it don't mat -

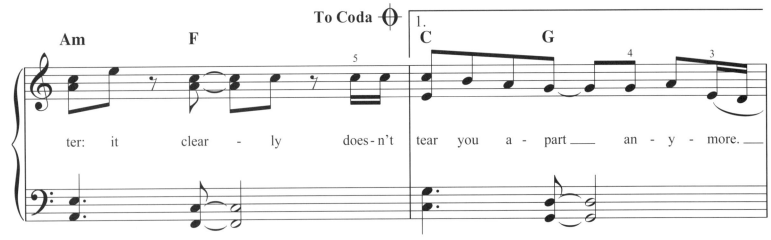

To Coda ⊕

1.

ter: it clear - ly does - n't tear you a - part __ an - y - more. __

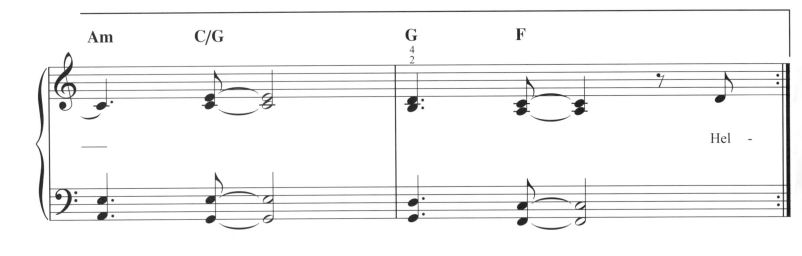

Hel -

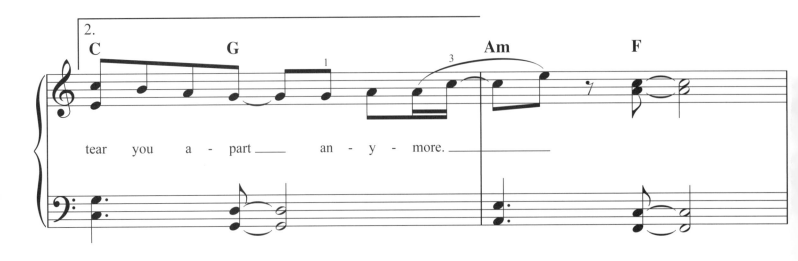

2.

tear you a - part __ an - y - more.

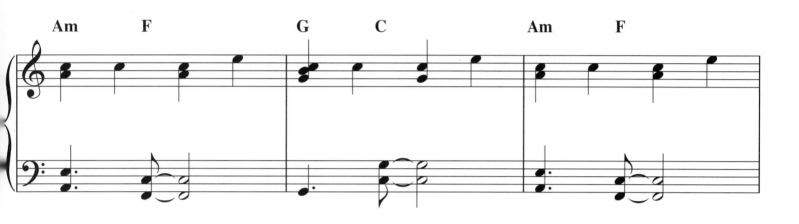

tear you a - part ____ an - y - more. ____

LET IT GO

Words and Music by JAMES BAY
and PAUL BARRY

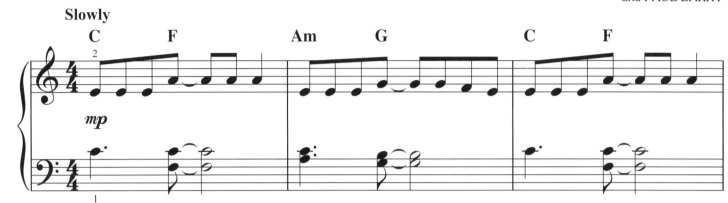

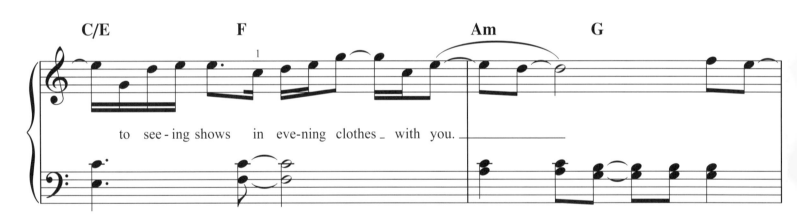

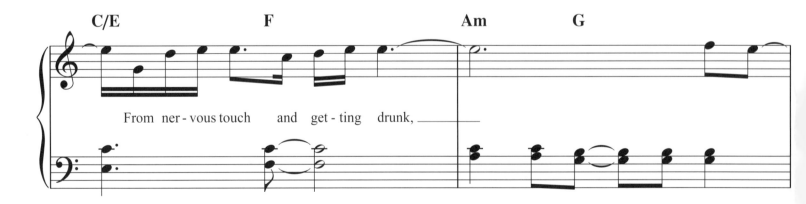

to stay-ing up   and wak-ing up ____ with you. ____   But now we're

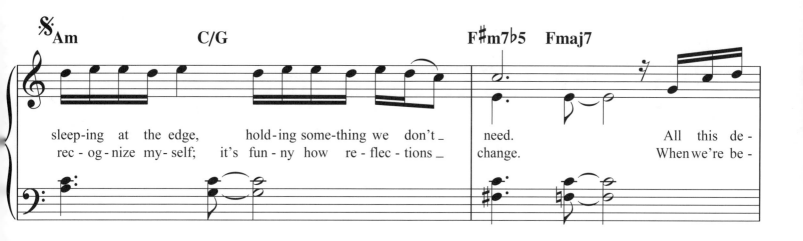

sleep-ing at the edge,   hold-ing some-thing we   don't _   need.   All this de -
rec - og-nize my- self;   it's fun - ny how   re -flec - tions _   change.   When we're be -

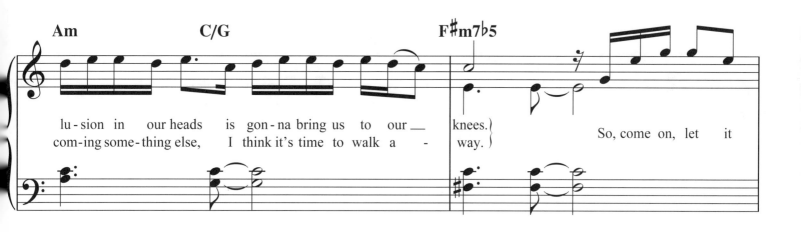

lu - sion in   our heads   is gon- na bring us   to our ___   knees.)   So, come on, let   it
com-ing some-thing else,   I think it's time to walk a -   way.)

go, _____ just let it   be. _____   Why don't you   be

you, _____ and I'll be me? Ev - 'ry - thing that's

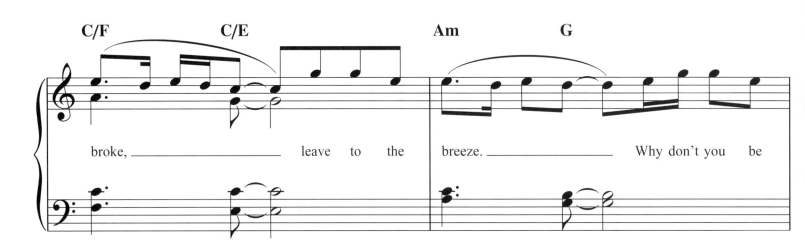

broke, _____ leave to the breeze. _____ Why don't you be

you, _____ and I'll be me? And I'll __ be me.

To Coda ⊕

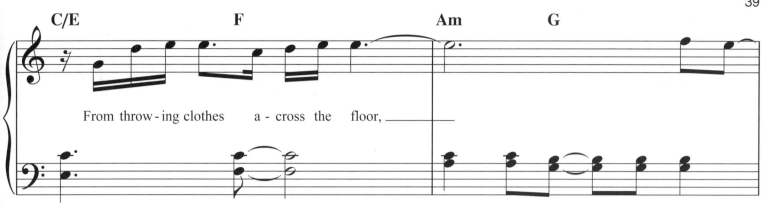

From throw-ing clothes a-cross the floor,

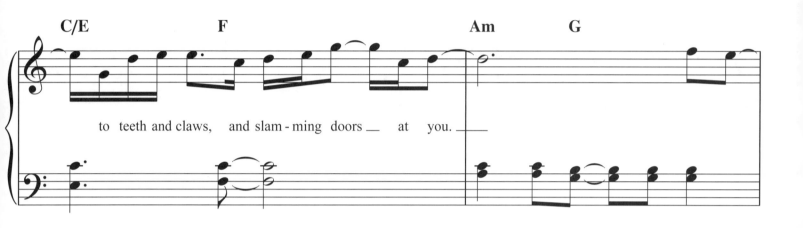

to teeth and claws, and slam-ming doors __ at you.

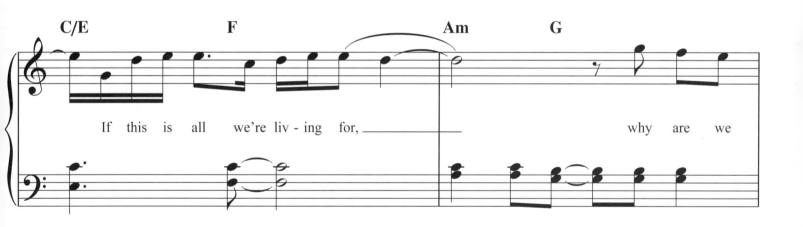

If this is all we're liv-ing for, __ why are we

D.S. al Coda

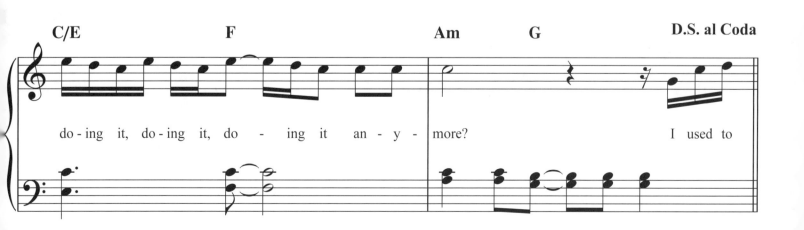

do-ing it, do-ing it, do - ing it an-y-more? I used to

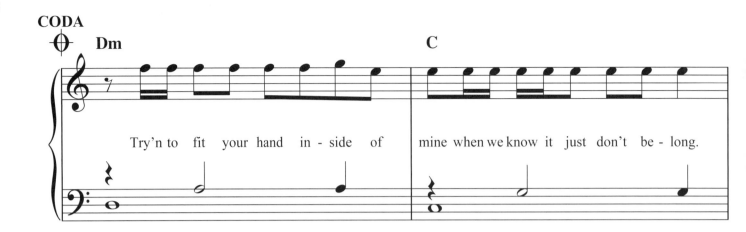

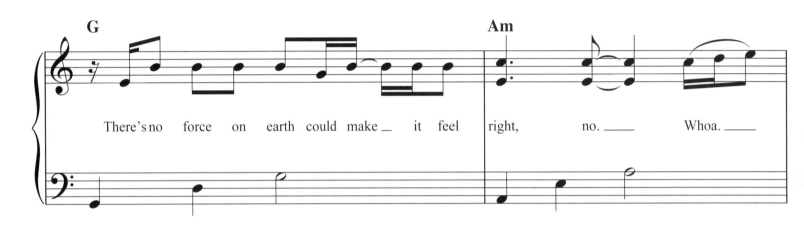

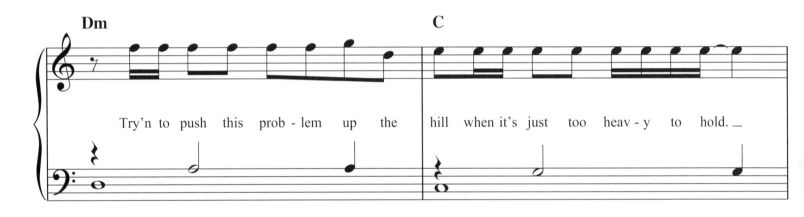

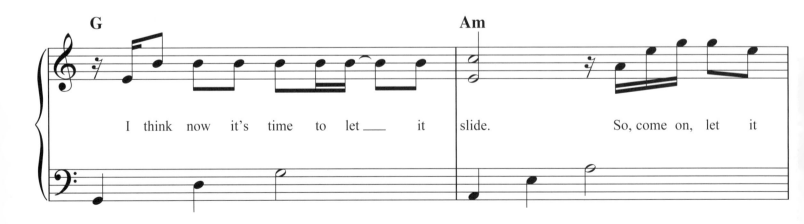

LIKE I'M GONNA LOSE YOU

Words and Music by CAITLYN ELIZABETH SMITH,
JUSTIN WEAVER and MEGHAN TRAINOR

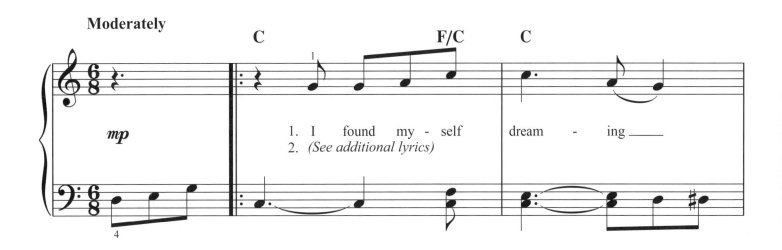

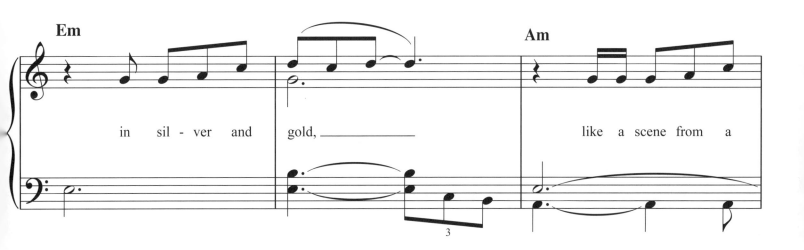

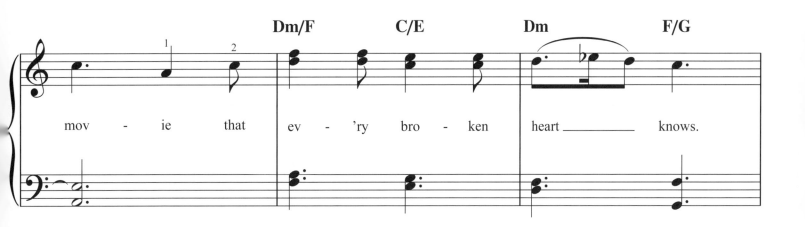

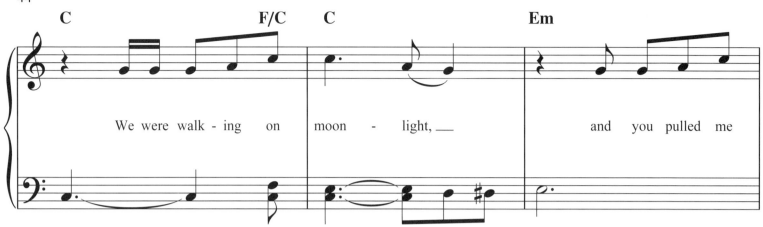

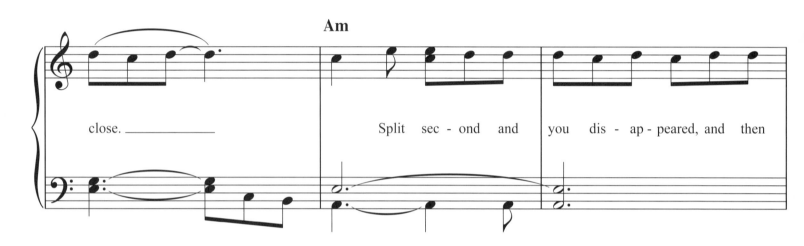

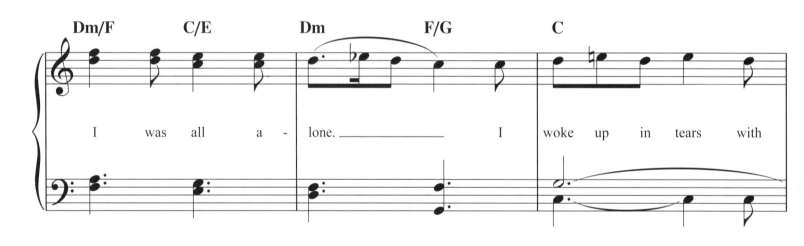

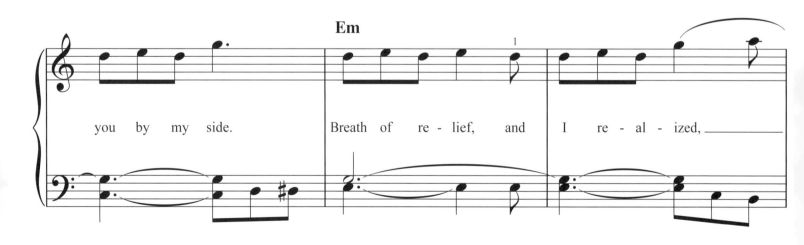

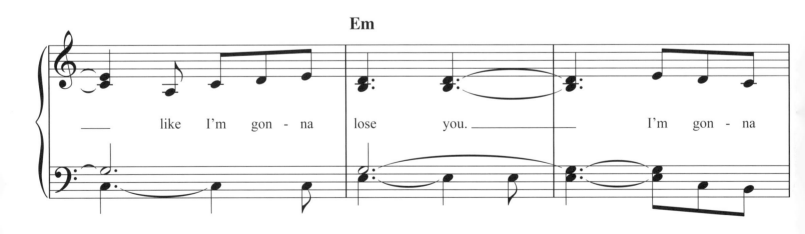

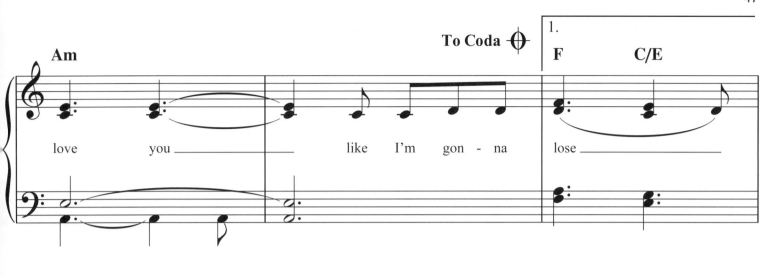

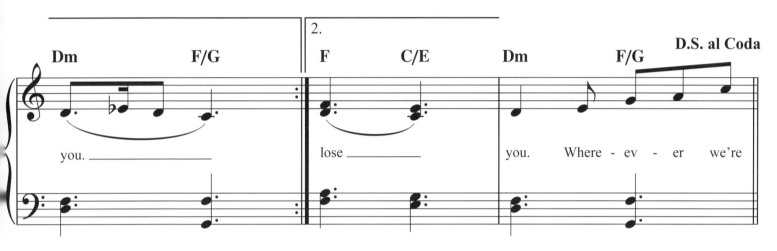

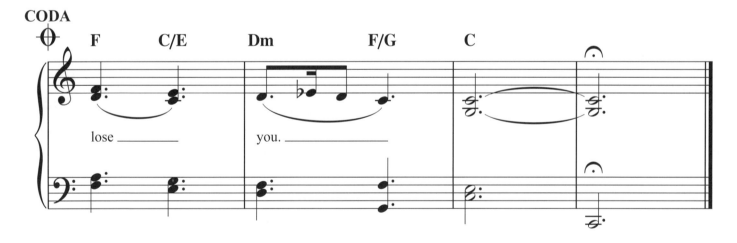

Additional Lyrics

2. In the blink of an eye, just a whisper of smoke,
   You could lose ev'rything; the truth is you never know.
   So, I'll kiss you longer, baby, any chance that I get.
   I'll make the most of the minutes and love with no regret.
   Let's take our time to say what we want,
   Use what we've got before it's all gone;
   'Cause, no, we're not promised tomorrow.

   I'm gonna love you like I'm gonna lose you.
   Love, ooh, lose you.

LOVE YOURSELF

Words and Music by ED SHEERAN,
BENNY BLANCO and JUSTIN BIEBER

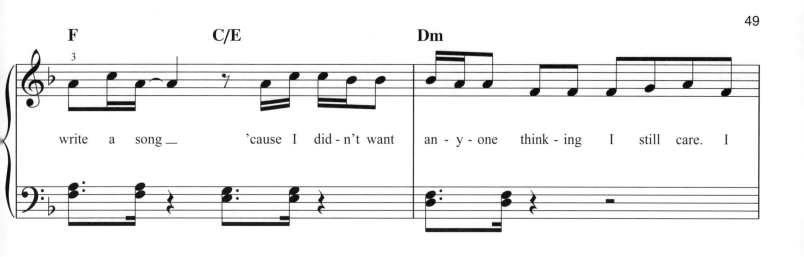

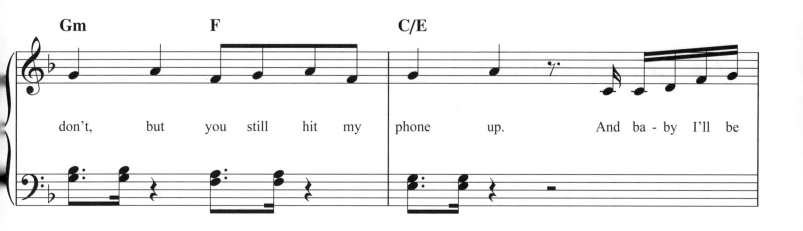

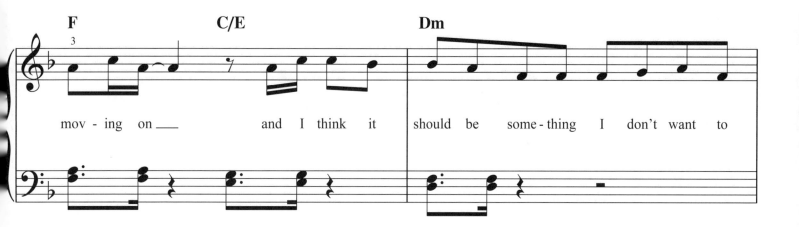

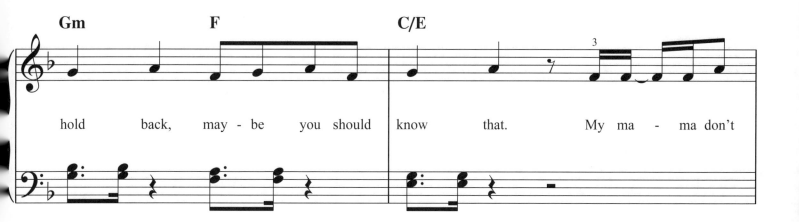

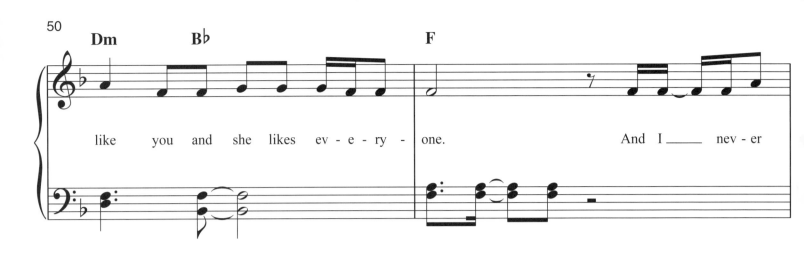

like you and she likes ev-e-ry-one. And I _____ nev-er

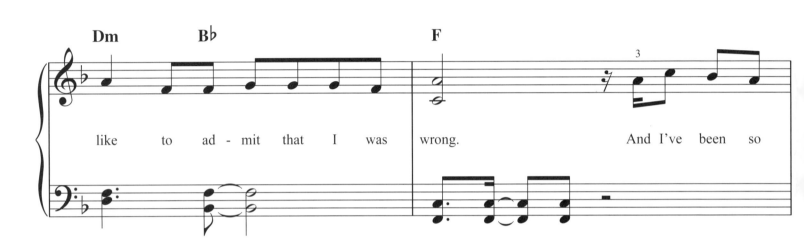

like to ad-mit that I was wrong. And I've been so

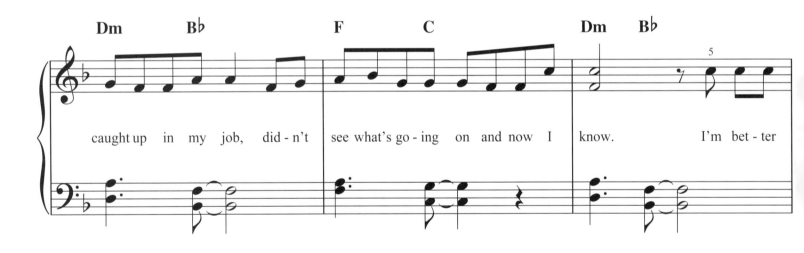

caught up in my job, did-n't see what's go-ing on and now I know. I'm bet-ter

sleep-ing on my own. 'Cause if you like the _ way you look that _ much, _ oh ba-by,

you should go and love your - self. ___ And if you think that _ I'm still

hold - ing ___ on ___ to some - thing you should go and love your - self. ___ But when you

1.

2.

Mmm. ___ Mmm. ___ Mmm, ___

___ mmm. ___ Mmm. ___ Mmm. ___

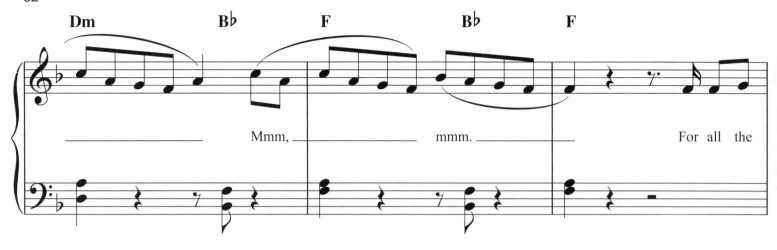

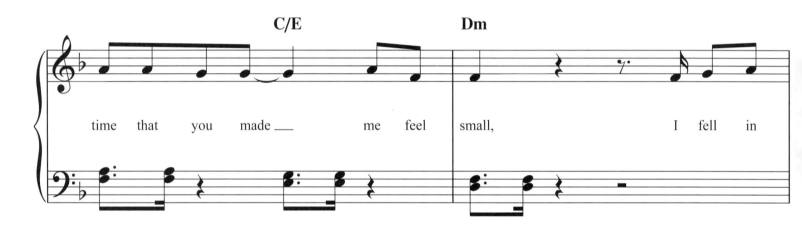

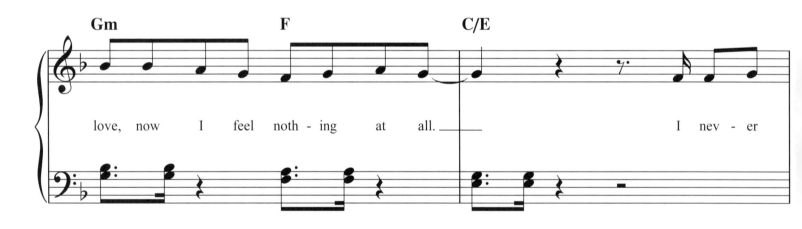

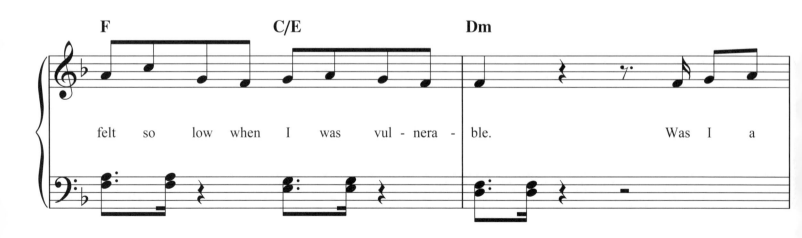

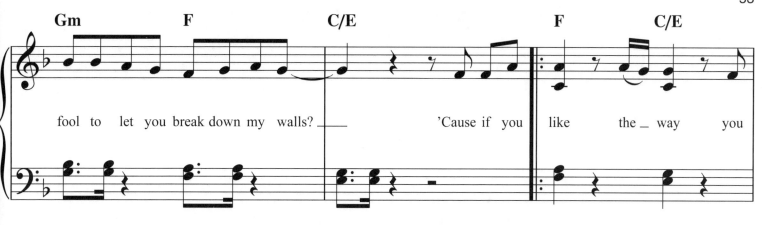

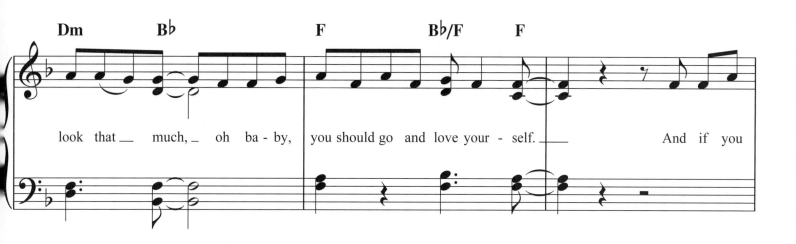

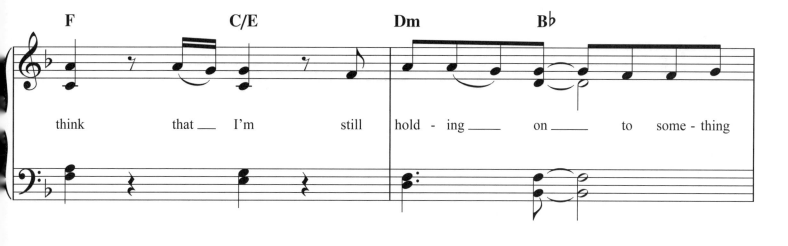

PERFECT

Words and Music by HARRY STYLES,
LOUIS TOMLINSON, JOHN HENRY RYAN,
JESSE SHATKIN, MAUREEN McDONALD,
JACOB HINDLIN and JULIAN BUNETTA

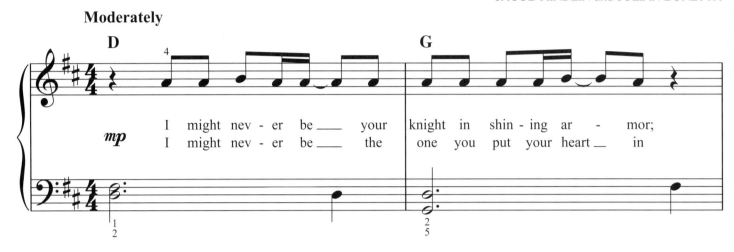

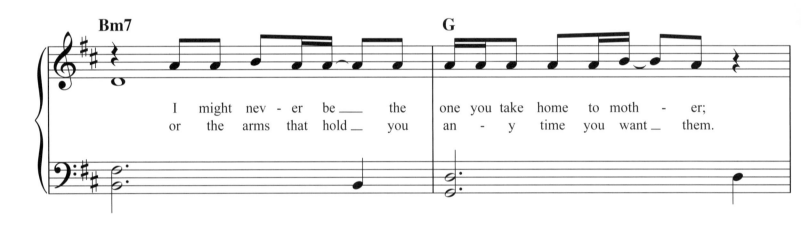

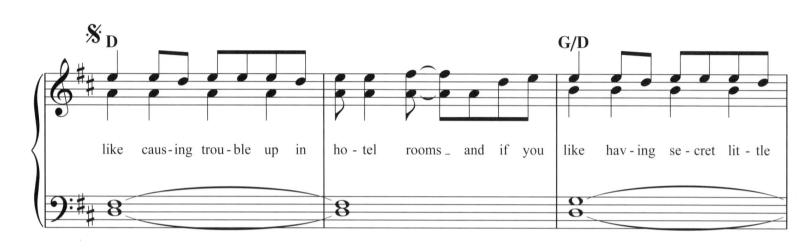

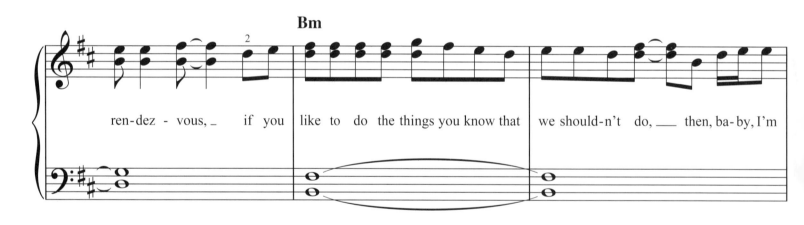

win-dows down _ and if you | like go-ing plac-es we can't | e-ven pro-nounce, _ if you

like to do what-ev-er you've been | dream-ing a-bout, ___ ba-by, you're

To Coda ⊕ | 1.

per-fect. _____ Ba-by, you're | per-fect, so let's start right | now.

2.

per-fect, so let's start right | now. _____ And if you | like cam-eras flash-ing ev-'ry

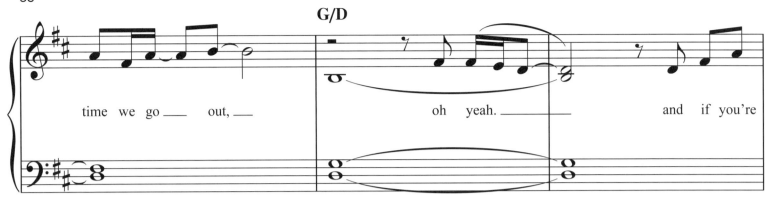

G/D

time we go out, oh yeah. and if you're

Bm

look-ing for some-one to write your break-up songs a-bout, ba-by, I'm

G   **D.S. al Coda**

per-fect. Ba-by, we're per-fect. If you

CODA

per-fect, so let's start right now.

SHE USED TO BE MINE

from WAITRESS THE MUSICAL

Words and Music by
SARA BAREILLES

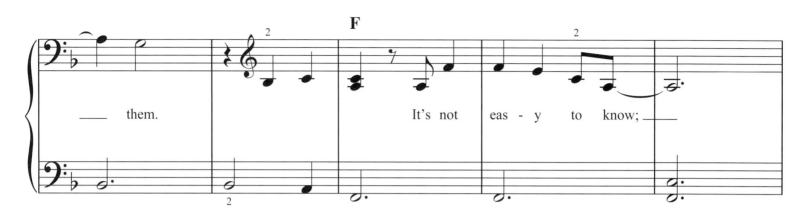

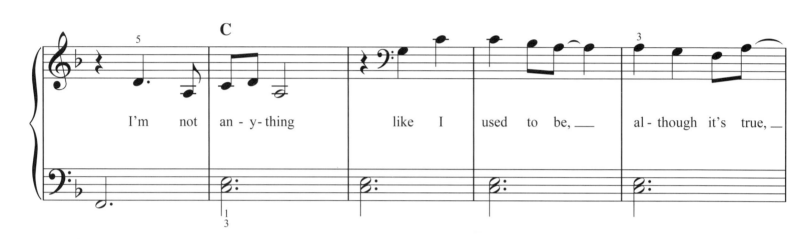

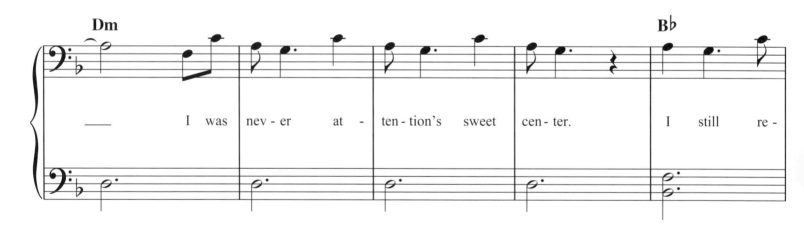

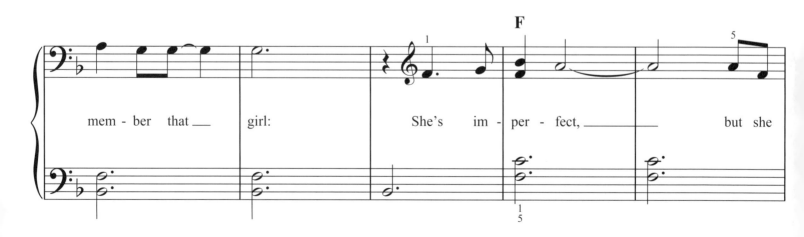

tries.   She is ___ good,   but she lies. ___

She is ___ hard ___ on her - self. ___   She is

bro - ken and won't ask for help. ___   She is mess - y, ___

___ but she's kind.   She is ___ lone - ly ___

most of the time. ___ She is all of this, ___ mixed up and

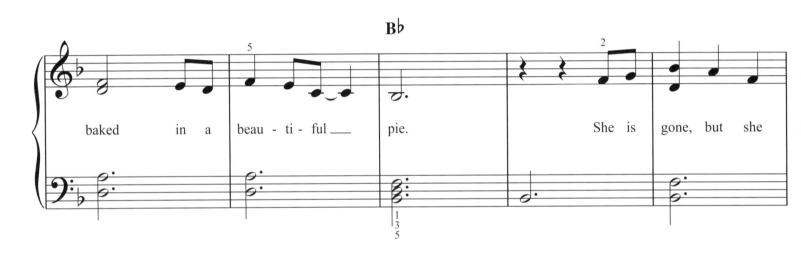

baked in a beau - ti - ful ___ pie. She is gone, but she

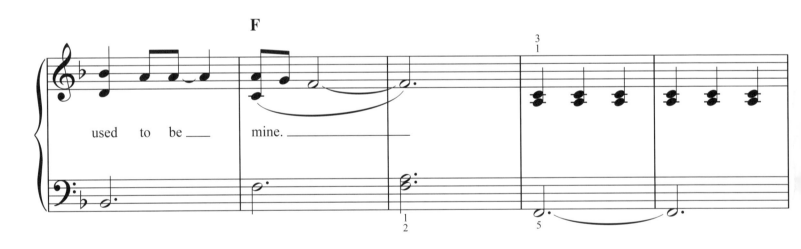

used to be ___ mine. ___

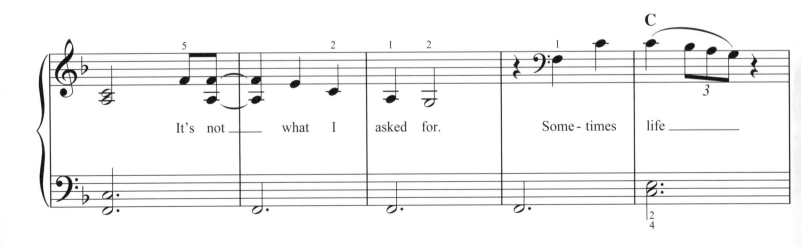

It's not ___ what I asked for. Some - times life ___

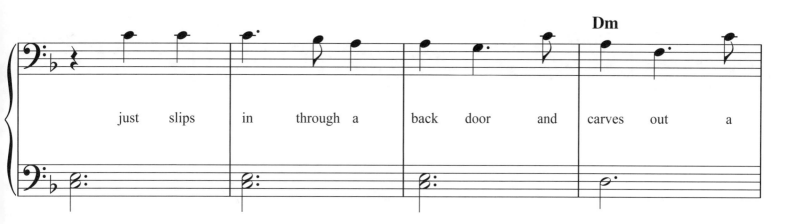

just slips   in   through a   back   door   and   carves   out   a

per-son   and   makes you   be-lieve _____   it's   all   true,   and

now   I've   got   you.   And   you're   not   what   I _____   asked   for.

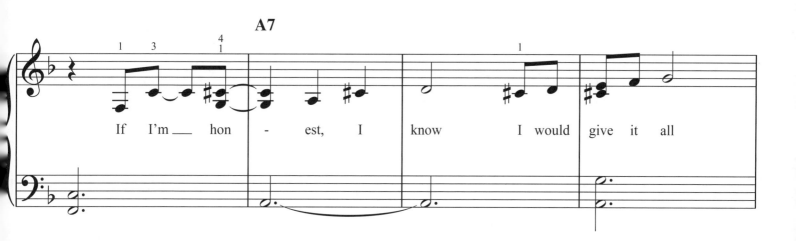

If   I'm __   hon - est,   I   know   I   would   give   it   all

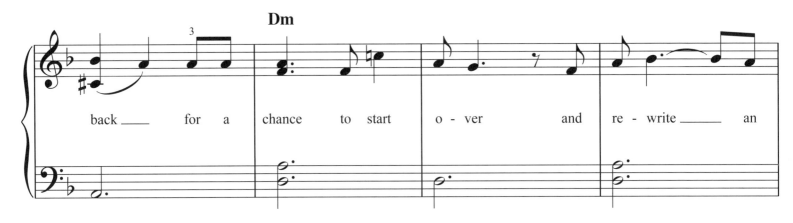

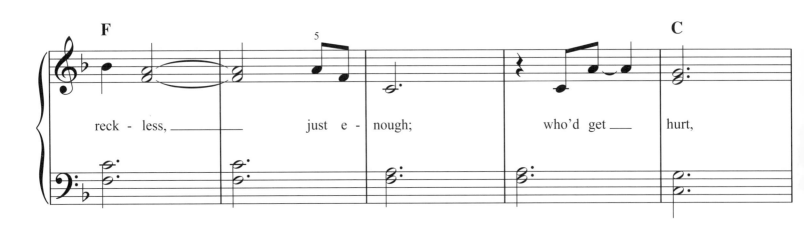

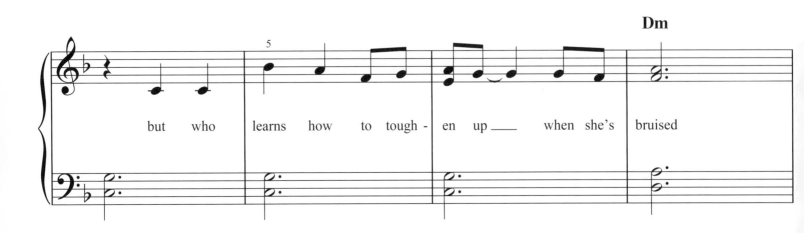

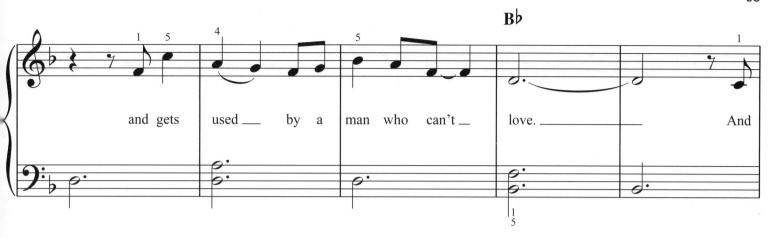

and gets used __ by a man who can't __ love. _____ And

then she'll get __ stuck, and be scared _____ of the life that's in -

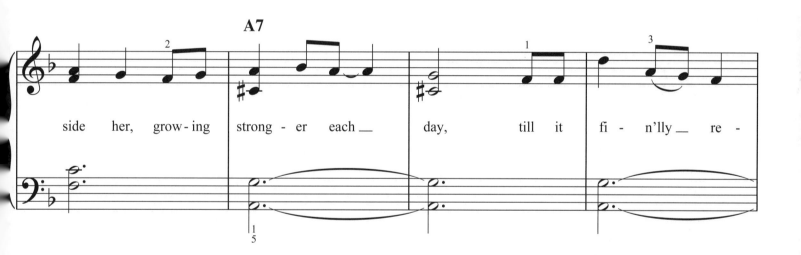

side her, grow - ing strong - er each __ day, till it fi - n'lly __ re -

minds her to fight just a lit - tle to bring back the fire __

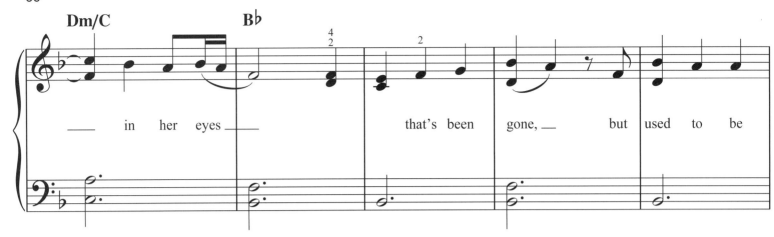

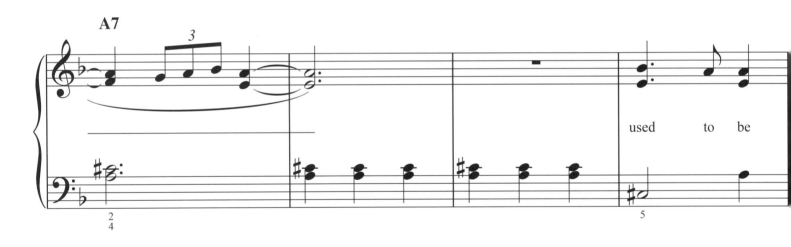

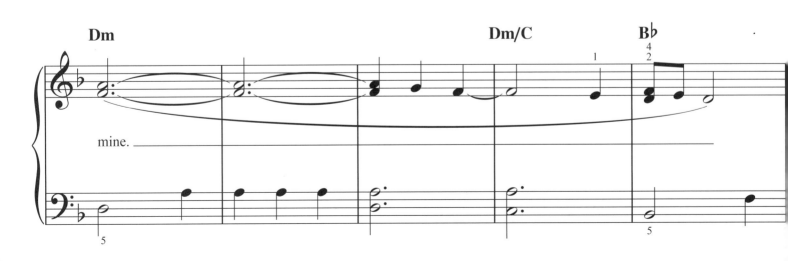

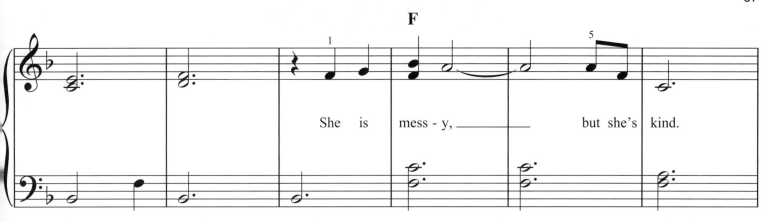

She is mess - y, ____ but she's kind.

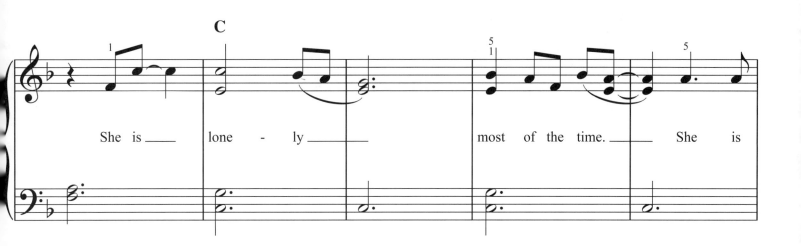

She is ___ lone - ly ___ most of the time. ___ She is

all of this, _ mixed up and baked in a beau - ti - ful _ pie.

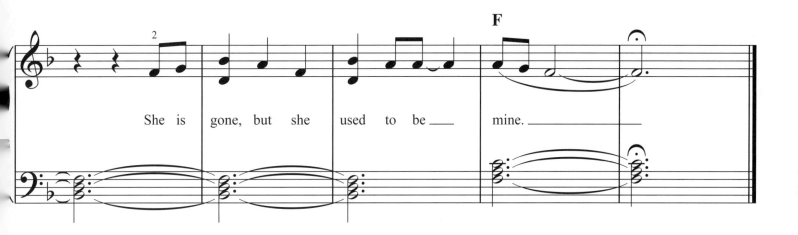

She is gone, but she used to be __ mine. ____

RENEGADES

Words and Music by ALEXANDER JUNIOR GRANT,
ADAM LEVIN, CASEY HARRIS,
NOAH FELDSHUH and SAM HARRIS

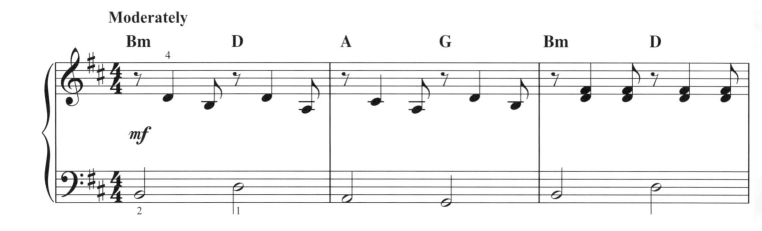

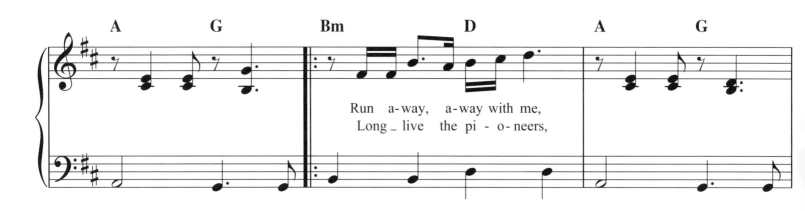

Run a-way, a-way with me,
Long live the pi - o - neers,

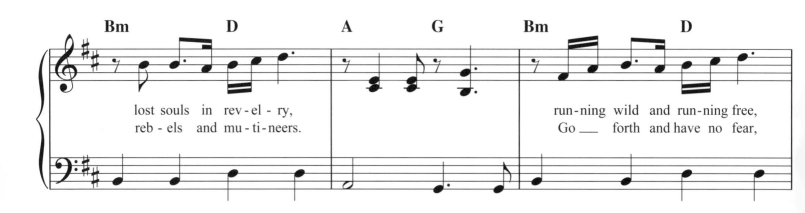

lost souls in rev - el - ry,
reb - els and mu - ti - neers.

run-ning wild and run-ning free,
Go forth and have no fear,

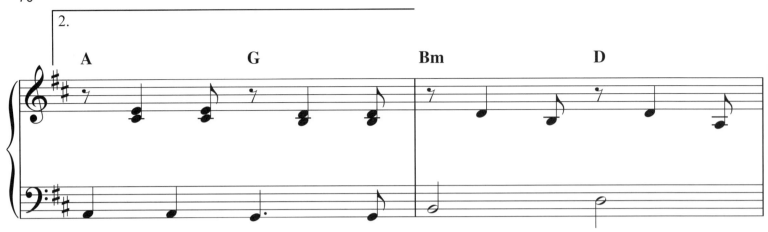

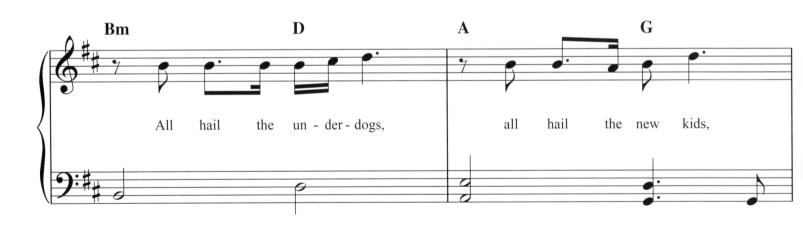

All hail the un-der-dogs, all hail the new kids,

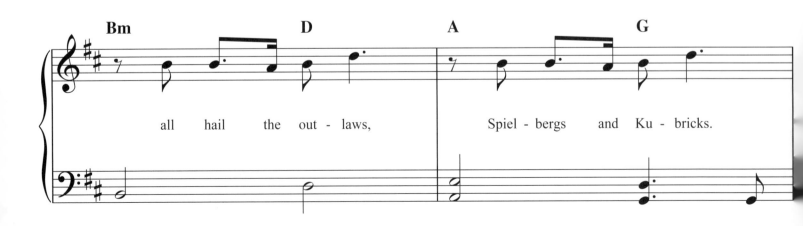

all hail the out-laws, Spiel-bergs and Ku-bricks.

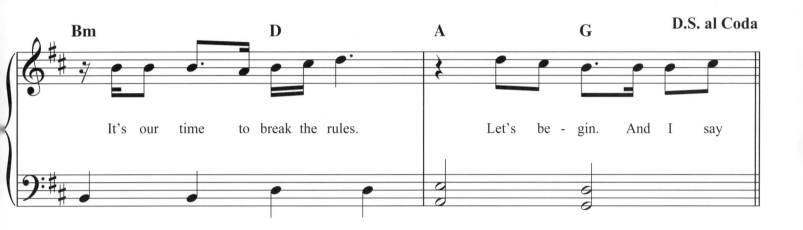

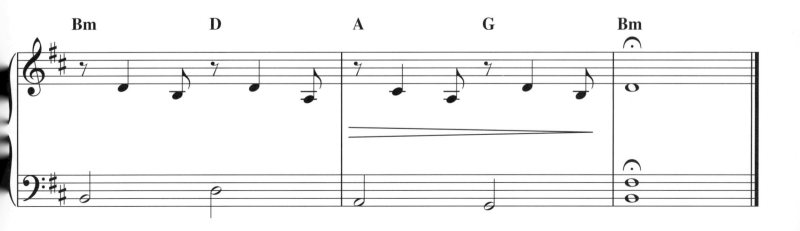

STITCHES

Words and Music by TEDDY GEIGER,
DANNY PARKER and DANIEL KYRIAKIDES

Moderate Latin groove

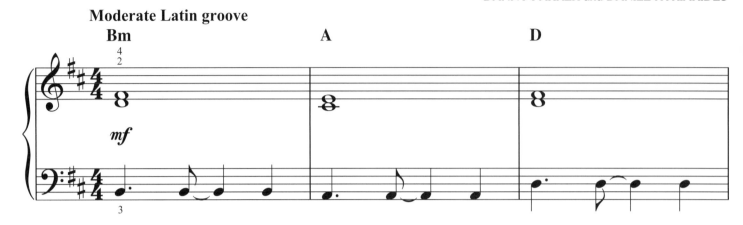

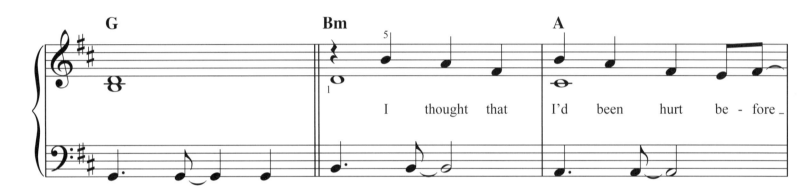

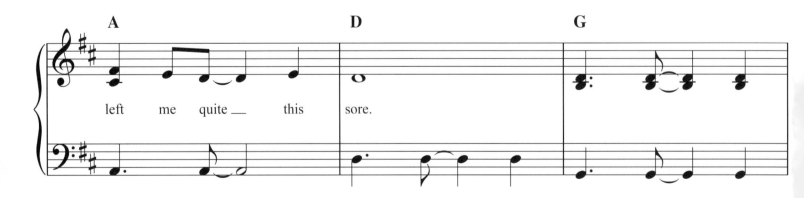

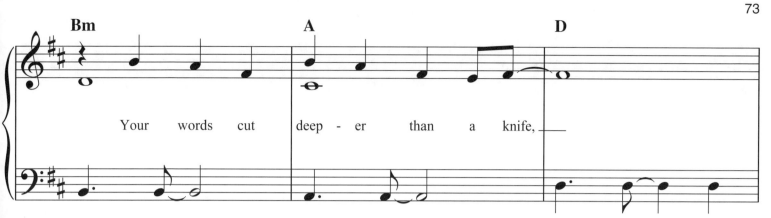

Your words cut deep - er than a knife, _____

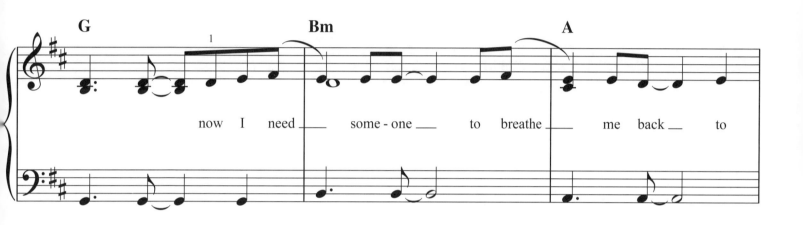

now I need ____ some - one ____ to breathe ____ me back ____ to

life.   Got a feel - in' that I'm

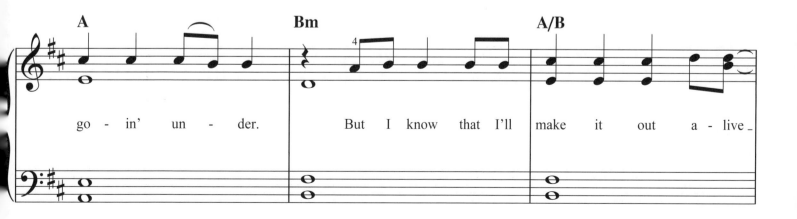

go - in' un - der.   But I know that I'll make it out a - live _

_____ if I quit call - ing you my lov - er and move on. _____

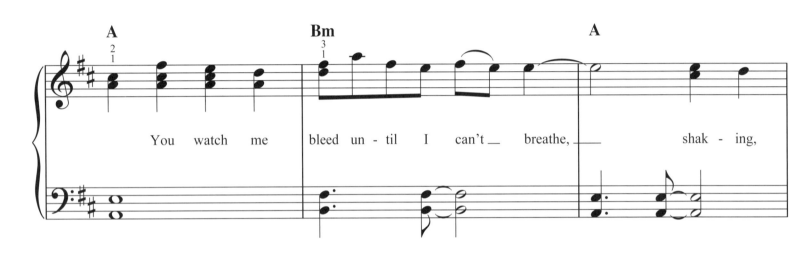

You watch me bleed un - til I can't _____ breathe, _____ shak - ing,

fall - ing on - to my _____ knees. _____ And now _____ that I'm with - out _____ your

kiss - es, _____ I'll be need - ing stitch - es. _____

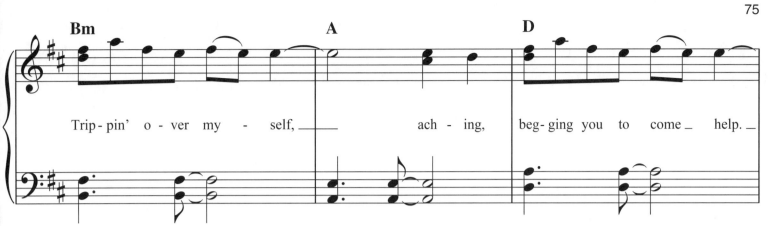

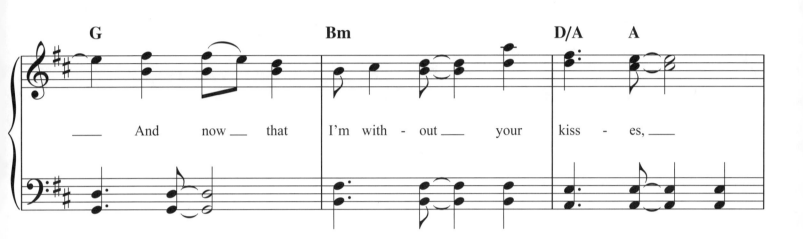

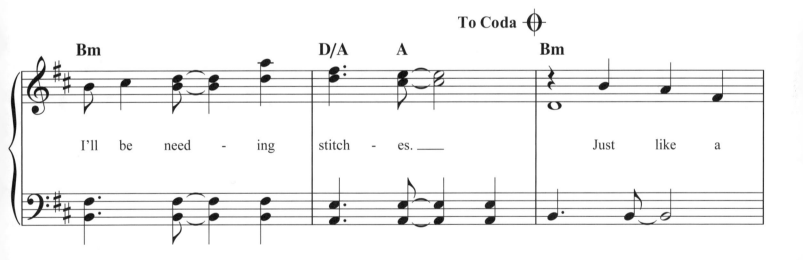

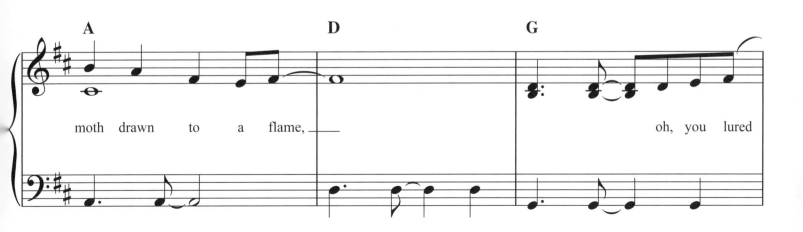

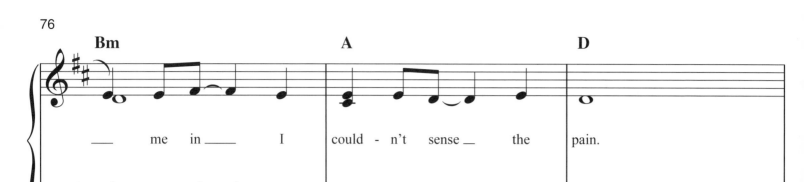

___ me in ____ I could - n't sense __ the pain._

_Your bit - ter heart cold to the touch. ___

____ Now I'm gon - na reap ___ what I ____ sow._

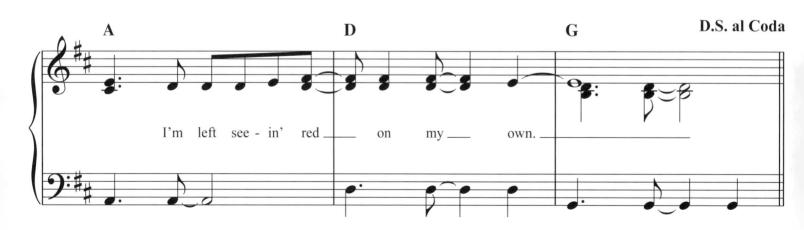

_I'm left see - in' red ___ on my ___ own. _____

D.S. al Coda

CODA

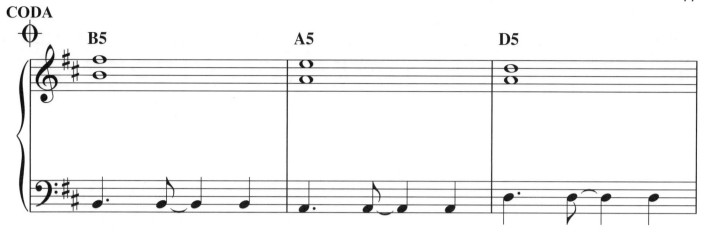

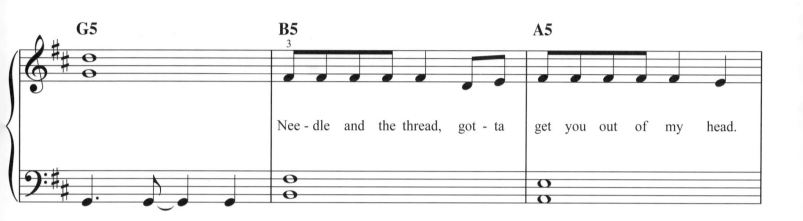

Nee - dle and the thread, got - ta   get you out of my head.

Nee - dle and the thread, gon - na   wind up dead.   Nee - dle and the thread, got - ta

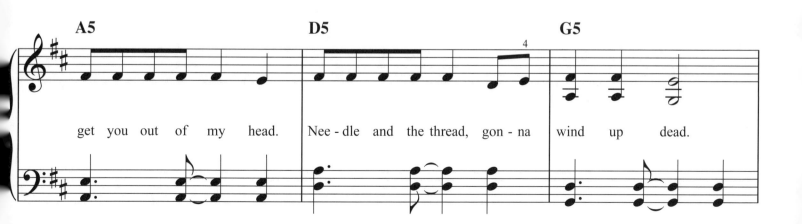

get you out of my head.   Nee - dle and the thread, gon - na   wind up dead.

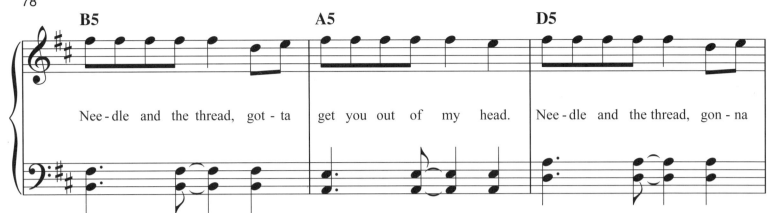

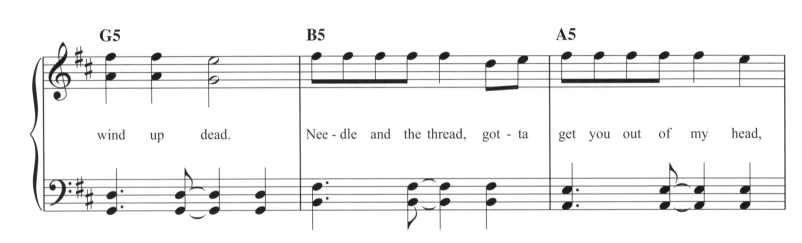

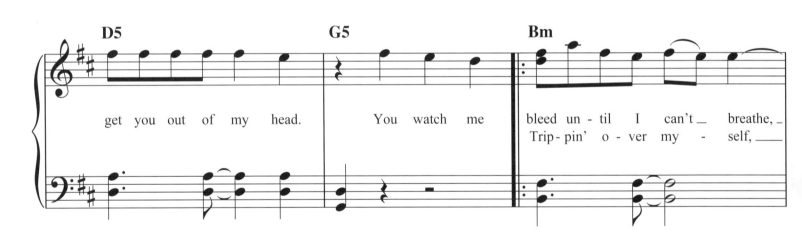

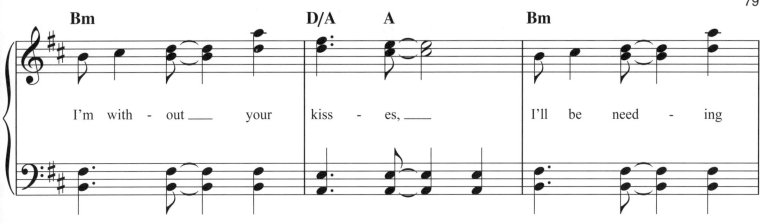

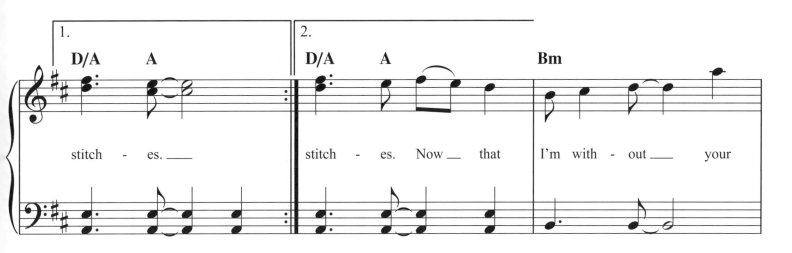

STRESSED OUT

Words and Music by
TYLER JOSEPH

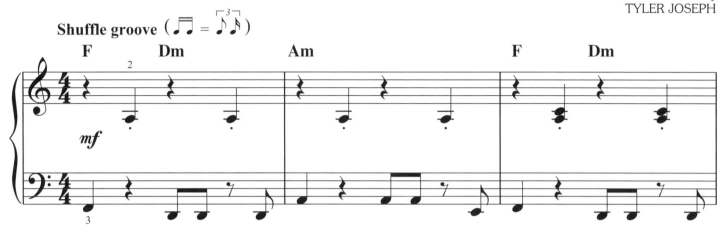

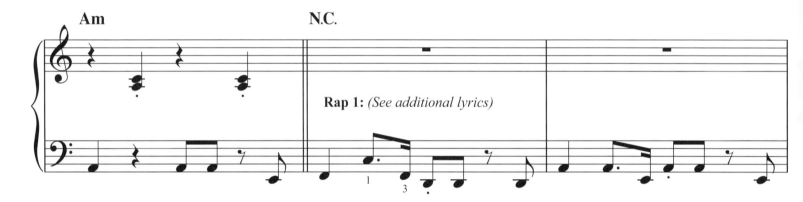

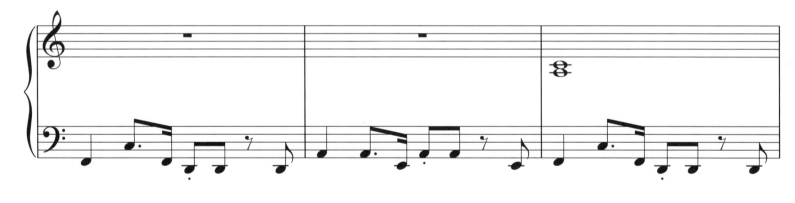

My name's Blur-ry-face, and I care what you think.   My name's

Rap 2: *(See additional lyrics)*

D.S. al Coda

CODA

C/E

E N.C.

My name's

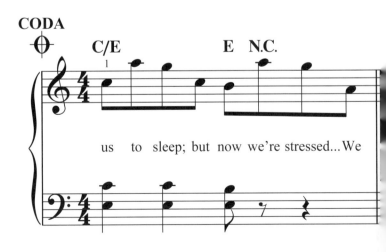

us to sleep; but now we're stressed...We

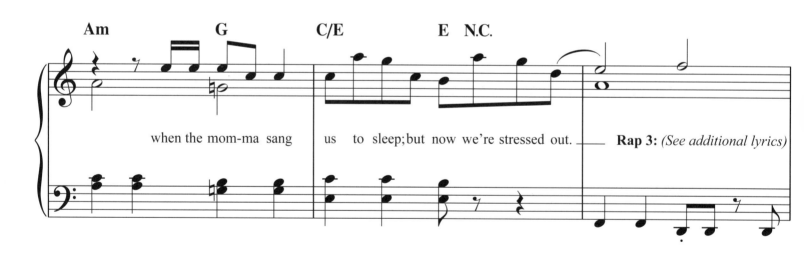

(Wake up! You need to make mon - ey!)

Additional Lyrics

Rap 1: I wish I found better sounds no one's ever heard.
I wish I had a better voice that sang some better words.
I wish I found some chords in an order that is new.
I wish I didn't have to rhyme every time I sang.

I was told when I get older all my fears would shrink,
But now I'm insecure and I care what people think.

Rap 2: Sometimes a certain smell will take me back to when I was young.
How come I'm never able to identify where it's coming from?
I'd make a candle out of it if I ever found it,
Try to sell it, never sell out of it. I'd probably only sell one.

It'd be to my brother, 'cause we have the same nose,
Same clothes, homegrown, a stone's throw from a creek we used to roam.
But it would remind us of when nothing really mattered.
Out of student loans and treehouse homes, we all would take the latter.

Rap 3: We used to play pretend, used to play pretend, bunny.
We used to play pretend; wake up, you need the money.
We used to play pretend, used to play pretend, bunny.
We used to play pretend; wake up, you need the money.

We used to play pretend, give each other different names;
We would build a rocket ship and then we'd fly it far away.
Used to dream of outer space, but now they're laughing at our face,
Saying, "Wake up, you need to make money?" Yo.

UMA THURMAN

Words and Music by ANDREW HURLEY,
JOSEPH TROHMAN, PATRICK STUMP,
PETER WENTZ, JACOB SCOTT SINCLAIR,
LIAM O'DONNELL, WAQAAS HASHMI,
JARRELL YOUNG, JACK MARSHALL
and BOB MOSHER

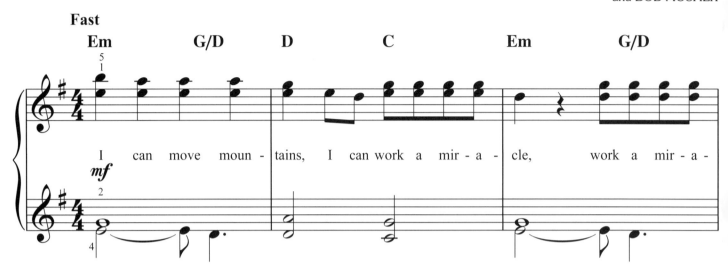

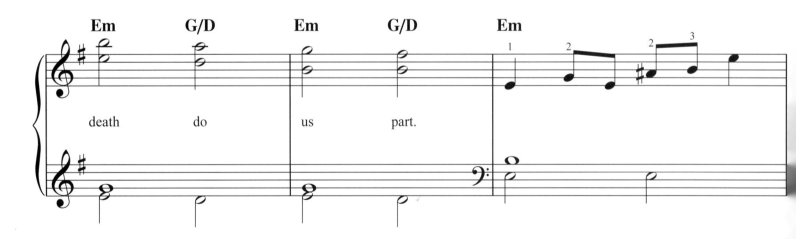

U - ma Thur-man and I can't get you out of my head. The / The

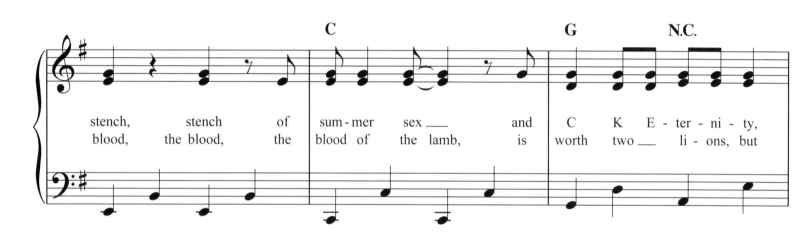

stench, stench of sum-mer sex ___ and C K E-ter-ni-ty,
blood, the blood, of the blood of the lamb, is worth two ___ li-ons, but

1.

oh, hell yes. ___ Di-vide me down to the small-est I can be.

Put your, put your v - v - ven-om in me. here I am. ___ And I

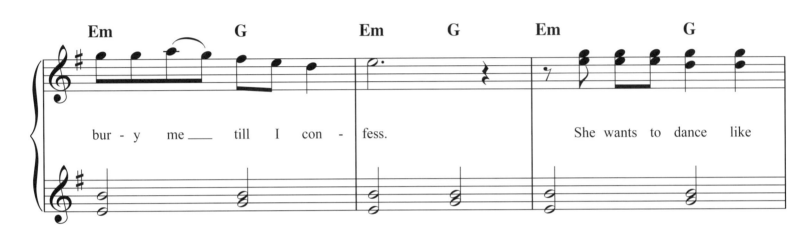

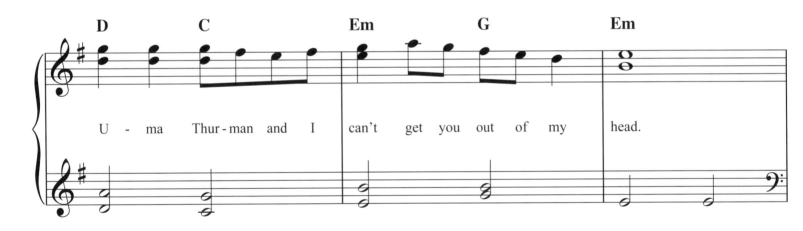

cle.   Oh,   oh,   oh,   keep   you   like   an   oath,   may   noth - ing   but

death   do   us   part.

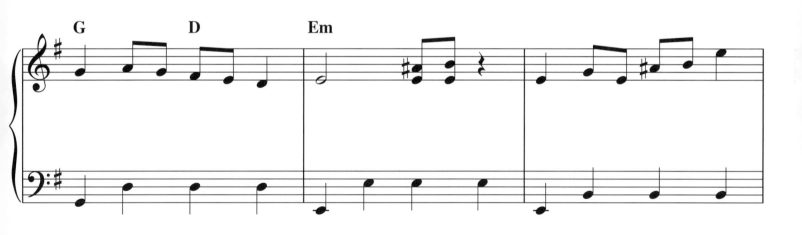

WRITING'S ON THE WALL

from the film SPECTRE

Words and Music by SAM SMITH
and JAMES NAPIER

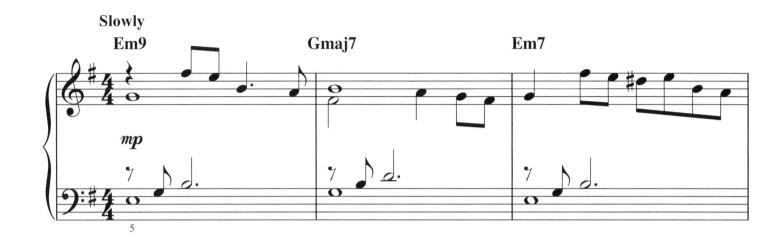

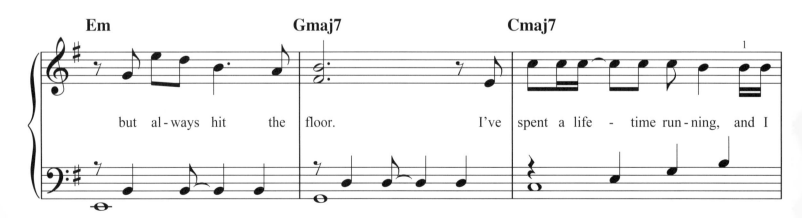

al-ways get a-way. __ But with | you, I'm feel-ing some - thing that | makes me want to stay. __

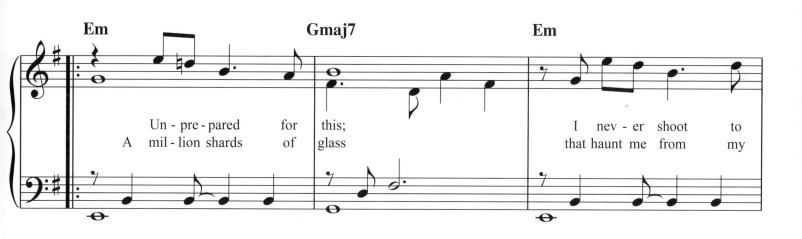

Un - pre - pared   for | this; | I nev - er shoot   to
A mil - lion shards of | glass | that haunt me from my

miss. | But I | feel like a storm is com - ing, if I'm
past. | As the | stars be - gin to gath - er, and the

gon - na make it through the day. __ And there's | no more use in run - ning,   this is
light __ be - gins to fade, __ when all | hope be - gins to shat - ter,   know that

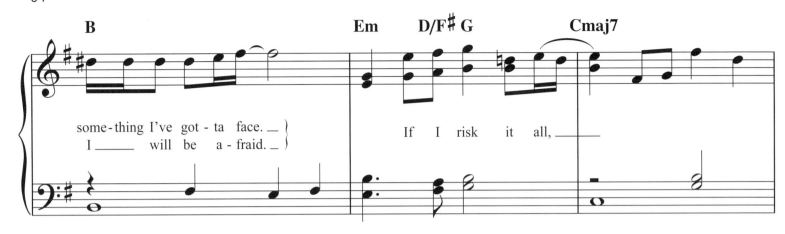

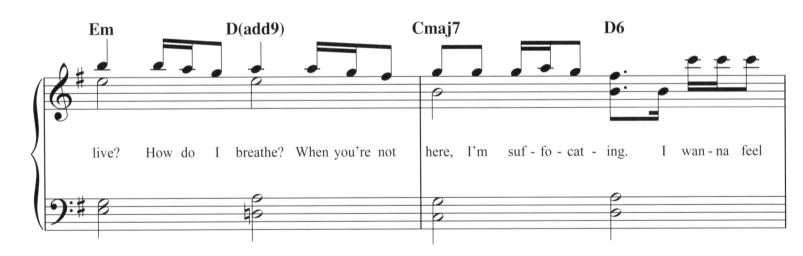

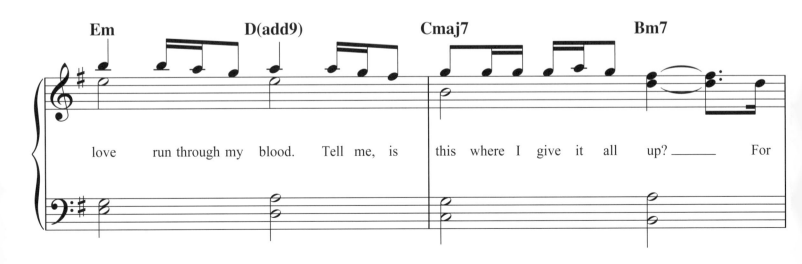